A WARDROBE FROM THE KING

A *Wardrobe*
FROM
THE KING

BERIT KJOS

VICTOR BOOKS®
A DIVISION OF SCRIPTURE PRESS PUBLICATIONS INC.
USA CANADA ENGLAND

This study guide is based on the *New American Standard Bible.*

Scripture quotations are from the *New American Standard Bible* (NASB), © the Lockman Foundation 1960, 1962, 1963, 1968, 1971, 1972, 1973, 1975, 1977, and are used by permission.

Recommended Dewey Decimal Classification: 227.5
Suggested Subject Heading: BIBLE, N.T.—EPHESIANS

Library of Congress Card Catalog Number: 87-62491
ISBN: 0-89693-419-5

VICTOR BOOKS
A division of SP Publications, Inc.
Wheaton, Illinois 60187

Are you battling guilt, discouragement, boredom, or fear? Do you long for relief as you face loneliness, rejection, hopelessness, and failure?

You may not be afraid to drive alone at night, but do you fear failure in meeting others' expectations, the loss of a friend, or lack of acceptance? Are you concerned about the physical, emotional, and spiritual safety of your children or loved ones? Perhaps your mind is bombarded with thoughts of inadequacy.

If any of these fears are as close to your heart as they are to mine, you need the protection of God's triumphant armor—a wardrobe from the King.

An invisible war of incredible dimensions has finally caught my attention. Day and night the enemy seeks ways to invade our space. Spotting the tiniest gap in our protective covering, he sneaks in to steal our joy, destroy our love, and shatter our peace. Stabbing at our vulnerable points, he devastates our thoughts, distracts our attention, and drains our strength.

If I thought my Shepherd, the sovereign King of the universe, would leave me for only a moment, I would tremble with fear; for the foe we face is far more vicious, clever, and powerful than any imaginary antagonist. Deadly arrows of doubt, discouragement, and despair speed toward their mark while the only Refuge from destruction beckons us to come into His shelter and share His victory.

Those who long for victory over fear, confusion, depression, or any other negative thought pattern cannot afford to be passive. Though it may seem unnatural to some women to don armor and fight a battle, God shows us that in the spiritual arena, gender makes no difference. No one is immune to enemy attack. Each man and woman must stand ready to fight every enemy to our peace, joy, and triumph in Christ.

Living in the safety of God's covering begins with understanding, affirming, and trusting in every piece of protective clothing He offers us. Through the delightful disciplines of worship, meditation, and prayer, we become more secure in a lifestyle of peace and confidence in the mighty, sovereign God.

CHAPTER ONE

CLOTHED BY THE

❧ PREPARING FOR BATTLE ❧

Are you tired of your old clothes? Have some of them worn so thin and threadbare that the wind blows right through? Do they make you feel less than beautiful?

How would you like to have a new wardrobe that radiates grace and beauty while protecting you in all kinds of weather? God has such an outfit ready, fitted and waiting for you. But His garments differ greatly from ordinary clothes. First, they are priceless. No payment could ever match their worth. Yet to you they are free; for your Father offers them as a gift and would be both disappointed and insulted if you insisted on paying for them.

Second, you put on His clothes from the inside out. They not only cover parts of your body on the outside; they become a part of you. They not only add color and texture to your appearance; they put a radiance in your face, a sparkle in your eyes, and new confidence in your countenance.

Finally, God calls this wardrobe armor, because it will protect you through every storm of life. It alone can guard you from spiritual, emotional, and physical attacks from invisible enemies both within and outside yourself—enemies to the peace, joy, love, hope, and victory which are yours in Christ.

For it is God Himself who covers you. By His armor, His life surrounds you, keeping you safe, close to Himself, and free to be His precious friend and trusted companion. Put Him on. He is your victory!

Precious Lord, please tell me more about this new set of clothes. Show me all its beauty and strength. Teach me how to put it on. Build in me an awareness of my need and a willingness to wear Your covering every day, so that I can be kept safe in You. Thank You.

Read Ephesians 6:10-18. Take time to thoughtfully reflect and ponder its message until it becomes part of you.

1. Why is this passage important to *your* life?

2. List all the exhortations (encouragements to do something) you find in this passage. Which exhortations are repeated? Remember that the enabling power of God's life comes with His commands.

3. What is spiritual warfare?

Read Ephesians 6:11-12.

4. Whether you are conscious of it or not, you are daily engaged in spiritual warfare. Who is your enemy in this battle? Describe his forces.

5. Consider the strategy of the enemy as described in 2 Corinthians 11:14-15 and Revelation 12:10-11. How does he attack *you*?

Were you involved in such a battle this last week?

6. Paraphrase and personalize Ephesians 6:10.

What does the phrase "in the Lord" mean to you?

How can you be *strong in the Lord* always?

Read Ephesians 6:14-17.
7. Look at the parts of the armor. Notice the verb tenses and list those pieces that have *already* become part of you.

If you are already wearing these pieces, when did you put them on?

8. What can you *do now* (every day) in order to realize the full protective power of these pieces of armor?

9. Which parts of the armor must you choose to put on each day?

10. In verse 18, what does God ask you to do? How does this verse deepen your awareness of our need for each other?

Read Exodus 17:8-13.
11. How was the Israelites' battle against Amalek won?

12

12. Relate the experience of Moses (his *need* in the battle and the support received) to your own battles. Do you need your brothers and sisters in Christ? Do they need you? Why?

13. What are some of the ways we encourage and strengthen one another *in Christ*? Give an example from your own life.

🦋 PUTTING ON HIS WORD 🦋

The storms began to hit hard at the end of my first year as a Christian. They took me by surprise. After a delightful year of learning to know Jesus and discovering the marvelous resources of His Kingdom, I thought I had a handle on the Christian life. Ignorant of spiritual warfare, I didn't guard against the perversity of my flesh (the old human nature) nor against Satan.

Suddenly neither my outward circumstances nor my inner struggles fit my vision of the Christian life. Disappointment, failure, and loss happens to everyone, but in me they opened the door to doubt and despair.

The questions in my mind reflected the confusion in my heart: *If God is my Shepherd, why doesn't He take better care of me? If God is my sovereign King, where is His power to provide strength and peace? If He is my Father, why isn't He gentler with me?*

Of course, the problem was me, not God. I just hadn't seen all that He offered me, nor had I applied all that He had shown me. My royal wardrobe hung unused in the closet.

I had pictured both a vertical love-relationship with my Lord (His hand and heart reaching down to me) and a horizontal friendship with Him (walking and working side by side). Both became real and precious to me, but I had missed the very best—the intimate union in which He and I become one.

Jesus gave an exciting description: "In that day you shall know that I am in My Father, and you in Me, and I in you" (John 14:20). In other words, my Father is first, Christ is in Him, I am hidden in Jesus, and Jesus fills me. Whatever touches me must first pass through both the Father and the Son. Not only does Christ cover me with Himself, but He and I become one. In His garments, I am not only protected, but I am also united with Him.

Are you ready and willing to put on Christ?

My royal wardrobe. I put on Christ, not by rote recitation of the parts of the armor, but by entering into a *relationship with the living God.* I secure my new set of clothes by a lifestyle of oneness and communion with Him. Both begin with a deep look at God.

As God reveals Himself to me in His Word made alive by His Spirit, I affirm all that He is to me. My sovereign, all-powerful King, who reigns over all (including the counterfeit powers of Satan), is not only the *whole* wardrobe, but He is also each individual *part.*

☐ He is *Truth,* the filter and reference point of all I see and hear, who has filled my pockets with priceless promises.

☐ He is my *Righteousness* who has cleansed and renewed me, so that I may stand spotless and beautiful before my King.

☐ He is my *Peace* who comforts me with the assurance of His sovereignty, wisdom, and love.

☐ He is my *Faith* who shields me from fear, doubt, and despair.

☐ He is also my past, present, and future *Salvation* who already saved me from guilt and condemnation. He saves me today from every trial and will one day exchange this decaying, earthly body for a fresh, new, beautiful body.

☐ He is the victorious *Word* with power to win every battle. He is everything I need to live, walk, and work triumphantly every day.

Dressing for victory. Having revealed Himself to me, God seeks a response. He longs to give me all that He is and has, but He can only fill and clothe me when I come to Him in trust, humility, and surrender. This attitude (so contrary to my human nature) comes readily when, by His Spirit, I "behold" Him (2 Corinthians 3:18).

When I see His greatness, I dare to trust Him, admit my need, and give myself to Him for the accomplishment of His purpose. Since words (thought, whispered, or spoken) confirm and strengthen the attitude of a yielded heart, I tell Him my response. For example, I might pray:

> Precious King, I trust You; therefore, I give myself to You as a living sacrifice. Transform me into Your image by the complete renewal of my mind, so that nothing will hinder me from seeing Your glory and knowing Your will. Hide me in Yourself, my Lord. Thank You for making us one.

Next, I *take* each piece of His armor by faith, *affirm* its basic truth, and *apply* it to myself:

> Thank You for Your truth. I will count on all the wonder-

ful things You have shown and promised me.

Thank You for Your *righteousness* in me. You have made me holy, precious and beautiful in Your sight (Isaiah 43:1-4, 25; Ephesians 1:4, 2:1-10).

Thank You for the *peace* I have in and with You. Keep me still in Your presence as we work together this day. Let Your peace flow through me to others (John 14:27, 16:33).

Thank You for the gift of *faith.* I will believe and proclaim Your sovereignty, wisdom, love, and triumph no matter what confronts me (Galatians 2:20).

Thank You for eternal *salvation.* I count on You to bring me safely and triumphantly through every challenge of this day. Keep my heart set on the encouraging hope of Your final salvation, which will bring me face-to-face with You, my King (Romans 5:8-10, 8:23; 1 Thessalonians 5:8-9; 1 John 3:3).

Thank You for Your *Word.* Show me which Scripture will bring triumph in my thoughts and emotions today (Ephesians 6:17).

As His protective presence becomes a growing conscious reality, only a few simple words may be needed:

Father, take me, I am Yours. Thy will be done. Keep me hidden in You. I love You, precious King. Thank you.

New clothes, new life. Assume that I have been coming to God each day with an attitude of trust and surrender. In fact, to "put on Jesus Christ" has become a daily habit. Even so, I find I am not immune to certain kinds of struggles. Why not?

It is essential to understand what God does and does not promise to do. If I presume that God's protection extends beyond His promise, I will become disappointed and frustrated. The truth is that His armor may or may not protect me against the storms of the world (Matthew 5:45). But it will always protect me against the assaults of Satan, whose arrows use the circumstances of the world to crush and destroy far more than could any storm.

In other words, God may not take me out of my circumstances, but He will bring victory in the midst of the trial. He will protect me against discouragement, despair, hopelessness, worthlessness—all the destructive emotions and thought patterns that rise up inside to disturb my peace, deny my resources in Christ, and quench my joy in Him.

Jesus asks me, "Will you go on with Me? Will you trust Me enough to remain hidden in Me? Will you continue to share My life?"

When He hides me in Himself, I become part of His life. I go where He goes. I share His heart, thoughts, concerns, and actions. Since Jesus has called me to oneness, I feel the winds that beat on Him. Together He and I face the storms and pressures of the world. Together we bear the stab of rejection. Together we share the pain of a friend and bring the comfort of truth.

If Jesus isolated me from all suffering, I could no longer be His friend and follower. He who is strong and I who am weak must walk together in His purpose. The very circumstances I would avoid, He now uses to make me a living, present-day proof of His triumph over the pressures of the world and the powers of Satan. Thus, the very storms that once brought devastation, now affirm the victory of the armor (1 Peter 4:12-13).

Standing together. "Love one another, even as I have loved you. . . . By this all men will know that you are My disciples, if you have love for one another" (John 13:34-35). Jesus reminds those who wear His clothes and share His vision of the importance of love.

Why is this love so important? Because we need each other. I may be able to get dressed alone, but without the support of faithful friends, I may become weary and find it unbearably difficult to "stand firm" in all that He is. Though our primary relationship is with Him, God made us to fit into one another's lives, to watch out, care, and pray for each other with the same concern that we have for ourselves.

Remember Paul's plea, the completion of his teaching on the armor:

> With all prayer and petition pray at all times in the Spirit, and with this in view, be on the alert with all perseverance and petition for all the saints, and pray on my behalf, that utterance may be given to me. (Ephesians 6:18-19)

When Satan directs doubt, discouragement, and fear at my weakest points, I need a friend who cares enough to prayerfully check my outfit to see that I am fully protected. When the missiles reach their mark and their venom distorts my perspective, I need a well-dressed friend who still sees clearly. Lifting each other up to God, we can stand together and demonstrate God's victory in every painful, confusing, and challenging situation.

❧*WEARING HIS WARDROBE* ❧

In the seventh lesson, we will study "the Sword of the Spirit which is the Word of God." However, now is the time to begin to collect the Scriptures that will win each battle for you. Remember that God's Word is the one offensive piece of the armor. While the other parts protect you from harm, only God's Word will silence the voice of the accuser and stop the attack.

Ask God to show you Scriptures appropriate to your personal battles. For example: To fight fear—Joshua 1:9 or Isaiah 41:10. For *any* circumstance—Galatians 2:20.

Write each verse on the front of a 3 x 5 card; put the verse reference on the back. Carry your collection of cards with you, and use any free moment as an opportunity to memorize and review them.

Whenever you experience disturbing or destructive thoughts, speak a Scripture truth that affirms God's victory. Be ready to share both Scriptures and victories with your group next week.

To become familiar with your swords, choose a verse each morning and meditate on it throughout the day. Use a personal notebook or journal to write your response to what the Lord shows you each day.

    DAY 1: Romans 8:37
    DAY 2: Ephesians 6:10
    DAY 3: Psalm 61:3
    DAY 4: Psalm 18:1-2
    DAY 5: Psalm 18:1-3
    DAY 6: Colossians 3:1-2
    DAY 7: Colossians 3:1-4

CHAPTER TWO

CLOTHED WITH

❧ *PREPARING FOR BATTLE* ❧

"What is Truth?"

Face-to-face with the Truth, Pontius Pilate asked this ageless question, then walked away. Soon afterward he condemned Truth to death. But God is Truth, and He reigns forever.

Truth is now at work in me, renewing my mind, transforming my soul, and making me one with my Lord. Truth clarifies, purifies, and cuts through all the distortion, deception, and compromise of the world.

"Clothed . . . with Christ," I am covered with Truth (Galatians 3:27). Through Him I see things as they really are.

Truth is the first piece of God's armor, the part that holds everything else together. I can go no further until I have "put on" the experiential knowledge of all that Christ will do through me. The truth of His character and all He has promised me is my protection in every conceivable circumstance.

God of Truth, I come to You. Teach me, fill me, surround me. Continue to "guide me into all truth," so that I might live in Your truth constantly. Thank You.

Read John 14:6.

1. Who is Truth?

2. Write the message of each of the following verses, replacing the word *truth* with the name of Jesus.

Psalm 51:6

19

John 8:31-32

John 16:13

John 17:17

Ephesians 1:13

3. Notice how the above verses fit together and build upon each
   other, then summarize their combined message. Which of the
   above verses means most to you today? Why?

Read 1 Chronicles 29:10-19. Examine David's beautiful prayer and
praise to God as he commissions his son Solomon to lead the people in
building God's temple.
   4. David really knows God! Look at your King through David's eyes.
      Then list His attributes. What does each mean to you? Appropriate
      these truths about God (make them part of yourself) by thinking

and meditating on them, then giving Him thanks—thus "girding your loins" with truth.

5. What happens when you recognize and affirm God's greatness together with your own finiteness? Are you encouraged? Explain.

6. Look at God in the following verses. How do you see Him? What do you learn about yourself. How precious are you to Him?

Psalm 139:1-16

Romans 8:31-39

Romans 11:33-36

2 Corinthians 3:4-6

2 Corinthians 12:9-10

7. In a practical way, how might you keep your "loins girded with truth"?

8. What are the two main aspects of truth (concerning God and yourself) that you must continually affirm before God?

Read 2 Corinthians 10:3-5.
9. Why and against what does the armor of truth protect you? What kinds of confusing or deceptive lies concerning you, your circum-

stances, or God might bombard you today?

10. Give a recent example of the protective power of Truth in your own life. How has He guarded you against Satan, the world, and the flesh?

11. What has occupied your mind this week? Look at these things or persons in the light of God's greatness and love for you. How does truth alter your perspective or your circumstances?

12. Review David's words of praise and affirmation to God in 1 Chronicles; then write your own prayer of praise to Him who is Truth.

13. Define *truth*.

❧ PUTTING ON HIS WORD ❧

Truth is like an assortment of strong, bright, multicolored threads that weave through each royal garment, binding them together. The individual pieces of my new wardrobe are:

> The *truth* of my King: His life in and around me.
> The truth of His *righteousness* shared with me.
> The truth of His *peace* in and with me.
> The power of *faith* in Truth.
> The truth of my three-fold *salvation*.
> The triumphant proclamation of the *Word* of Truth.

To make this truth vital and active in my life I need to take the following steps:

☐ FEED ON TRUTH—read, study, and delight in God's Word.

☐ MEDITATE ON TRUTH—review truths stored in my mind, hide them in my heart, and make them part of myself.

☐ FILTER FOR TRUTH—screen every idea and retain only those that agree with God.

☐ FOLLOW TRUTH—walk by its light, bringing every action as well as thought into harmony with truth.

When I follow these four steps, I wear a beautiful, effective expression of my identity in Him.

Feed on Truth. Contrary to the way I usually dress, I put on truth from the inside out. Inner health produces outward beauty. Therefore, I put on Truth by feeding in the green, fertile pastures of the Bible. Here I see, hear, and learn to know precious Truth; for when *I seek God in its pages,* He opens my eyes to see Him in His manifold glory. I hear my Father assure me of His eternal, unconditional love for me. I become intimately acquainted with my best Friend, and I learn to live in union with my beloved Bridegroom who is preparing me to share His life for all eternity.

Here I read God's love letters to me. Chapter after chapter discloses His purpose, His ways, His joys, His sorrows, His amazing love, His awesome holiness, His sensitive heart. This is our time together—a time of listening and being heard, a time of loving and being loved.

Having heard His voice and received strength and direction for my day, I begin work, confident that my King who spoke truth to me will indeed accomplish all that He has promised.

Meditate on Truth. Having "put on" truth by feeding on God's Word, I determine to wear truth each moment of my day. In his letter to the Colossians, Paul shows me how to meditate:

> If then you have been raised up with Christ, keep seeking the things above, where Christ is seated at the right hand of God. Set your mind on the things above, not on the things that are on earth. For you have died and your life is hidden with Christ in God. (Colossians 3:1-4)

Biblical meditation is quiet reflection on God's Word and works, and careful attentiveness to His ways. It involves focusing my spiritual eyes on God's glory and waiting for Him to reveal Himself. It is choosing to let my heart speak His own thoughts (from His Word) back to Him, and then listening for His gentle voice in my heart revealing more of Himself.

It is receiving the "meat" of God's Word, "swallowing" it, then (as a cow chews its cud) ruminating on God's wisdom and goodness. It is repeatedly bringing His marvelous truths back to conscious thought, ever richer in the light of the Spirit.

I put on truth as I put off old fleshly thoughts and hold on to God's thoughts. Day by day I repeat this process until wearing truth becomes as natural as breathing. Self diminishes as the Initiator of thoughts and actions lives increasingly in and through me—thinking, speaking, acting, and being the beauty of truth—so that others may see and know Him through me.

God's words in the Old Testament show me how to wear truth and live in His triumph:

> His delight is in the law of the Lord, and in His law he meditates day and night. And he will be like a tree firmly planted by streams of water, which yields its fruit in its season, and its leaf does not wither; and in whatever he does, he prospers. (Psalm 1:2-3)

Oh, how I love Thy law! It is my meditation all the day.
(Psalm 119:97)

When I remember Thee on my bed, I meditate on Thee
in the night watches; for Thou hast been my help, and in the
shadow of Thy wings I sing for joy. (Psalm 63:6-7)

Filter for Truth. Sometimes it seems impossible to keep my mind "set
on the things above." An overwhelming onslaught of distracting, negat-
ing thoughts (reflecting fear, failure, worthlessness, and hopelessness)
crowd out His thoughts of love, peace, and victory. How do I ward off
these intruders and nurture the peaceful, triumphant truths of my
King? God gave the answer through Paul:

> For though we walk in the flesh, we do not war according
> to the flesh, for the weapons of our warfare are not of the
> flesh, but divinely powerful for the destruction of fortresses.
> We are destroying speculations and every lofty thing raised
> up against the knowledge of God, and we are taking every
> thought captive to the obedience of Christ. (2 Corinthians
> 10:3-5)

Since the first challenge to the reign of truth comes in my thoughts, I
must make a choice. Will I yield to the "flesh" and its way of thinking?
Or will I continue to let truth fill and renew my mind, conforming it to
the mind of my King?

Jesus sees, thinks, and acts truth. So must I, when I abide in Him.

My own thoughts express worry, hurry, and resentment—all sorts of
lofty speculations which contradict the truths I know about my King.
But when my Lord, the sovereign, omnipotent God of the universe, has
planned my life, why should I worry? When my Shepherd has all the
time in the world, why should I feel hurried? When my Father's love
guides my relationships and His justice will ultimately reign, why
should I ever be resentful?

When I question the source of a thought, God's written Word and
His indwelling Spirit show me the course to take:

1. If the thought is from the flesh, I must *deny* it and *put on* the truth
   that fits my new identity in Christ. I must replace "I can't do it"
   and "I'll never be able to forgive that person" with "I can do
   everything through Him who gives me strength" (Philippians
   4:13).
2. If the thought is from Satan, I must *resist* his lie by the power of
   Jesus, then *replace* it with truth.

3. If the thought is from the Spirit, I must *affirm* and *obey* it, then *walk* in the light of that truth.

I dare not be spiritually lazy and neglect truth. The moment I yield my mind to the perspectives of self or the world, I drop the armor. God's thoughts are higher and better than my own; mine don't even fit in His wardrobe. I cannot rest in Him while I think the thoughts of the world. But the armor stays in place when His Word filters my thoughts and I view all things from the purifying perspective of truth.

Follow Truth. Each day Truth whispers, "Will you choose my thoughts and ways. Do you really want to be my companion? Then come and follow. Share my concerns, my sufferings, my work and my life."

If I wanted His new clothes in order to look good, or if I seek the armor merely to find comfort and safety, I might answer yes to His call, but my fellowship with Him would be short-lived. Soon I would discover that His path through the world involves deprivation and pain. Choosing the lifestyle of Truth, oblivious of the full nature and purpose of the armor, would bring complaints and resistance when He brings me into battle.

I persevere today because I know that none of the world's suffering can compare to the joy of oneness with Him. If I, like Paul, have set my heart on the King and have made Him my first love, I will not hesitate when Truth beckons me onward. Like Paul, I have found the treasures of my heart and can "count all things to be loss in view of the surpassing value of knowing Christ Jesus my Lord" (Philippians 3:8).

Truth, like meat, makes me strong and healthy when I take the right steps: choosing the good rather than the bad, taking it home, storing it in my mind, then eating it. If, over the years, I have bought and stored that which is counterfeit or corrupted, I need to cleanse my mind of the old junk food and fill it with fresh growth-producing truths.

God does not evaluate my life by what He sees in the pantry of my mind; His main concern is how I use what I have. He knows what I have stored. My pantry may be full of food as a Christian who has been collecting truth for years, or it may hold only a cupful as in a new believer. Now He watches to see *what I eat;* for the food that I chew and swallow into my heart determines my thoughts and actions. In turn, my thoughts and actions determine the protection of oneness with my King—or the pain of separation from Him.

For years I filled my mind with information that was both inconsistent with my knowledge of God and destructive to my relationship with Him. I chewed, swallowed, and filled my mind and heart with junk food, then suffered the consequent destructive thoughts and actions—

sins which separated me from my King.

One day I saw the danger of this process and began to clean and fill my pantry with good things—wonderful truths about God, His character, and His ways. Every morning I read His Word. I even chewed and swallowed some as I stored it away on the shelves of my mind.

If I had stayed with His food all day, I would have avoided a bellyful of distress. Instead I patted myself on the back for the good breakfast, opened the newspaper, and swallowed some of its facts. I watched TV for a while, put some of its tidbits on a shelf, and ate the rest.

A phone call brought reminders of a hurtful incident still stored in my mind. That became an early supper. Rather than satisfying me, the meal only whets my appetite. So I reached for some more snacks: thoughts of a "hopeless" situation, a confusing relationship, a rejection by a friend.

Suddenly I felt the pang of indigestion. What did I eat? Where is that good meat I bought yesterday? I reached for it, but the hunger was gone. In choosing my own way, I had lost my sense of direction and missed the joy of His presence. Why didn't I just eat the food He gave me?

Depleting my pantry is certainly no worry, for whatever I eat is replaced and increased by its very use. Just as the fish and bread were multiplied to feed five thousand people, so that which is consumed is multiplied in my pantry—whether it is good or bad.

What will *you* eat? Jeremiah tells his choice: "Thy Words were found, and I ate them, and Thy words became for me a joy and the delight of my heart" (Jeremiah 15:16).

Let us encourage each other to seek, choose, take, and feast on Truth—restorative truths that renew our minds, transform our souls, and produce strong, vibrant, triumphant life that never ends.

❧ WEARING HIS WARDROBE ❧

Ask God to give you a deep awareness of what kind of information you receive and feed on each day. What do you store in your mind? What do you "eat"—take into your heart, where it can influence your thoughts, will, and emotions? Does it come from God, the world, or your flesh?

Copy this chart into your personal journal and fill it in each day. Write the various types of input you received, the effect each input had on you, and your response. Practice the responses that bring victory and peace. You may want to review the three points mentioned in "Putting On His Word" before you begin.

	INPUT	ITS EFFECT	MY RESPONSE
FIRST DAY:			

CHAPTER THREE

CLOTHED WITH *Righteousness*

❧ *PREPARING FOR BATTLE* ❧

Relationships and responsibilities crowd my mind and stir my heart. Television, newspapers, people, and possessions tempt me to focus on everything but my King. How can I escape their tyranny? How can I manifest the purity of the King while living in an unholy world? How do I maintain a sense of personal worth when my performance points to failure? In this age of abundance, how do I discern between wants and needs, between lust and genuine Spirit-inspired responses to my Father?

Quietly Jesus seems to whisper, "Seek first My kingdom and My righteousness, then I will choose for you my very highest and best. Look first at Me, then I will share with you My true perspective of the world and its treasures, of circumstances and their significance to your growth, and of people and their part in your completion. Infinitely happy are those who hunger and thirst for righteousness, for they shall find complete fulfillment."

The hungry and thirsty know their need. Nothing can stop them from seeking until they find the source of life-giving sustenance. Satisfied, they yearn for more as Jesus salts their hearts and produces perpetual thirst and satisfaction. Having glimpsed His loveliness and experienced His sufficiency, they find no fulfillment apart from an ever-deepening oneness with the Fountain Himself.

Our Lord is a holy God who cannot tolerate sin, yet He loves the sinner. (That's you and me apart from Him!) Only by His mercy, grace and righteousness can we enjoy the greatest gift of all—life in His holy dwelling place and the peace of His constant presence. What a privilege!

Precious, holy King, I can neither come to You, hear You, nor please You on my own. I need You every moment. My heart longs for deeper oneness with You

*in all that You are, do, and desire; I yearn to understand more
clearly and to appropriate more fully the gift of Your righteousness. Thank You
for leading me on Your paths of righteousness, my King and my Shepherd.*

Read Psalm 84. Delight in God's nearness as you pray His words back
to Him.
 1. Which part of the psalm is most meaningful to you? Why?

 2. Verses 11-12 present two conditions for living life in His holy
    dwelling place. Explain what each means to you.

    How do these two conditions relate to righteousness?

 3. In each of the following verses, what does God show you concern-
    ing righteousness? Take time to *reflect, apply* each to yourself, and
    tell God your response.

    Matthew 5:6

    Matthew 6:33

    Romans 5:17

    1 Corinthians 1:30

Read Philippians 3:7-10.

4. Paraphrase and personalize verses 8 and 9, making this message your own.

5. What is meant by "the righteousness which comes from God on the basis of faith"? (v. 9)

Read Romans 4:3-5, 18-22.

6. What *action* on Abraham's part was credited to him as righteousness?

7. Describe Abraham's faith.

Read Romans 3:21-24.

8. True righteousness comes from ＿＿＿＿ through ＿＿＿＿ and is available to ＿＿＿＿ . Why can confident assurance of these truths make a great difference in your life?

9. When and how did you receive the righteousness of Christ? Take time to consider the cost and to give Him thanks.

Read Ephesians 6:14.

10. Because you were "crucified with Christ," He now lives in your innermost being. He has made you one with Himself; therefore, you are righteous in Him! Although you already have received His righteousness, what action on your part makes it an effective part of your armor?

11. Even though you already are righteous in Christ, you must always be ready to deal with any hindrance to the free expression of His righteous life in and through you. What does His breastplate protect you against?

Read 1 Thessalonians 5:8.
12. Explain how the "breastplate of righteousness" and "the breastplate of faith and love" are in harmony with each other.

13. Look up the following Scriptures and write the steps to the practical, experiential righteousness that brings peace and victory.

Matthew 18:33-35

Romans 6:11, 13

Ephesians 4:22-24

1 Thessalonians 5:16-18

14. In order to make the *full armor* a practical reality, practice putting on each part. How can you keep your "loins girded with truth"?

How do you put on and wear "the breastplate of righteousness"?

Why is the sequence of these two parts important?

Read Psalm 23.
15. What does God promise you concerning righteousness?

How are you encouraged by the above promise?

What must you do in order to allow Him to make this promise true in your life? See also John 10:4.

16. When and how did your Shepherd lead you in His "paths of righteousness" this week?

❧ PUTTING ON HIS WORD ❧

I once felt guilty ... without hope ... a failure. But not any more! There is now "no condemnation for those who are in Christ Jesus" (Romans 8:1). The accuser may still hurl his cruel charges against me, but I refuse to allow his barbs to grow and consume my thoughts. I will no longer abuse myself with self-condemnation. Jesus pronounced me free, innocent, righteous, and holy.

Like Paul, "I am convinced that neither death, nor life, nor angels, nor principalities, nor things present, nor things to come ... shall be able to separate us from the love of God, which is in Christ Jesus our Lord" (Romans 8:38-39). If God loves me that much, how could I ever feel insignificant or worthless?

When I understand the truth of Christ's righteousness in me, a new confidence transforms my attitude toward myself, my King, and all other persons in my life. When I really know who I am, I can no longer depreciate myself or depend on affirmation from people. When I claim my new identity, I don't need to compete, criticize, feel inferior, or prove my worth by performance. God's righteousness frees me to love, affirm, forgive, and protect others. I can rejoice with their successes, weep with their sorrows. I dare to risk rejection and loss for the sake of my King and His friends.

In other words, when I accept and appropriate His righteousness, Jesus makes it a vibrant reality in my life. Freed from the bondage of insecurity and insignificance, I can live His life of selfless love, which is the essence of righteousness and the fulfillment of all His commands. His life then becomes the fragrance of my life.

Accepting His righteousness. Since God has challenged me to believe that I am righteous in Him, I must trust and believe what He has told me, in spite of all contradictory evidence and contrary feelings.

It is not up to me to be righteous; I can never please Him on my own. But Jesus is my righteousness; He chose me, died for me, cleansed me, covered and filled me with His righteous resurrection life.

Today's challenge to believe in Him for righteousness has three parts—past, present, and future. I am already righteous by His life in me. He lives in me moment by moment to express His righteousness through me in every circumstance, and I believe that "in the future there is laid up for me the crown of righteousness, which the Lord, the righteous Judge, will award to me on that day"—that wonderful day when I will meet Him face-to-face and be fully transformed into His likeness (2 Timothy 3:8).

Until that great day, I must wear my breastplate of righteousness, affirming with my mind and will what I know in my heart about my King. I must count on His spotless life covering me through every challenging circumstance. He then guards my heart from Satan's painful accusations of failure and worthlessness, while He keeps me free to channel His righteous life of love first back to Himself, then to those around me.

Meeting the challenge. How would you respond if a newspaper reporter writing a human interest story asked you the following question: "Tell me, do you consider yourself righteous, pure, and holy?" Would you hesitate to tell the truth, fearful that he would consider you arrogant, dishonest, or crazy if you answered yes?

I often find it easier to think and speak the lies of the world than to speak God's truth and risk appearing foolish or proud. But I will never win the battles of the kingdom while conforming to the thinking of the world. Trusting and speaking truth wraps His covering securely around me. Denials and disbelief leave me uncovered and vulnerable to enemy attacks.

Jesus' life, not mine, determines my righteousness, and nothing can separate me from Him. Then why don't I always enjoy fellowship with my King? Why does He sometimes seem so far from me? And why doesn't His righteousness always shine through my lifestyle? Because I don't always think and act in harmony with the truth He has given me.

Practicing righteousness. Some days I still measure righteousness by my performance rather than accepting it by faith. I ignore the truth of God's righteousness in me in favor of another truth: His desire that righteousness be manifested through my every thought, word, and action. I regress to believing what I see and feel, not what I know; consequently, I lose the power to be all that God has made me.

What happened? How do I reconcile these two facts: I am already righteous; yet day by day I am learning to live a righteous life.

God tells me that I became a new person, holy and beautiful in Him, the moment I believed and received His life. But doubt will prevent me from wearing His beauty and purity from day to day. No failure can keep His love from flowing *toward* me, but disobedience will hinder the flow of His love *in* and *through* me.

Therefore, God has planned a way to build faith and obedience in me. This life-long process is characterized by a succession of trials, failures, victories, growth, and plateaus.

Notice the balance between *my part* and *His part* in this process:

> Just as you have always obeyed, not as in my presence only, but now much more in my absence, work out your salvation with fear and trembling; for it is God who is at work in you, both to will and to work for His good pleasure. (Philippians 2:12-13)

I "work out" my salvation by faith and obedience. When I affirm the truth of His righteousness in me, it shines through my life in increasing measure, for the old ways no longer fit. When I yield myself to Him in obedience, He takes over "to will and to work in me." There will be inner battles—I will find myself doing what I hate and failing to do what I should. Yet I will continue to pursue the King's lifestyle because, in the light of my new identity, I can no longer be comfortable in my old flesh patterns.

Wearing His righteousness. I enter a lifestyle of righteousness the same way I put on the rest of the armor—through an attitude of worship. Jesus wills the renewing of my mind and the transformation of my soul into His likeness—a process fed by affirmation and application of truth.

The four steps that help me put on truth will also clothe me in His righteousness:

☐ FEED on the truth of His righteousness. His Word reminds me of His death which freed me, His blood which cleansed me, His resurrection life which empowers me. I can delight in His unwavering love and acceptance. I must not be harder on myself than God is. I can adopt His attitudes toward me by memorizing Scriptures such as Isaiah 43:1-4, Jeremiah 31:3, and Romans 8:31-39 that affirm my precious worth to Him.

☐ MEDITATE on His truths which renew my mind and transform my heart. I can delight in all that I am and have in Jesus.

Years ago, during a time of discouragement, I made a commitment to meditate on the above affirmations for one month. Morning, evening, and often during the day, I reviewed these transforming truths and suddenly discovered that they had renewed my mind. Since then, I have never doubted God's love nor my worth to Him.

☐ FILTER for truth, permitting only those thoughts that agree with truth. By replacing negative thoughts with thoughts that affirm my relationship with God, I will remember that to Him I am pure and beautiful. God, my only Judge, sees me clothed in Christ, declares me acquitted from guilt and free to live forever in His holy presence.

☐ FOLLOW truth, allowing His righteous life in me to direct and empower every thought and action. I can choose an attitude of worship as the basis of my lifestyle.

Perfecting love. Because the life of Jesus fills and surrounds us, you and I are equipped to live His life of self-giving love. We are ready to be one in Him. This oneness not only protects us from loneliness, rejection, competition, and inferiority, it also weakens the enemy. For when God's people stand together, firm in their King, ready to fight for (and alongside) one another, doors slam shut to Satan so that he cannot gain entrance.

Until I choose to lay down my self-oriented life and put on His life of unselfish love, the feelings and will of the flesh will dominate my choices. Like a railroad engineer choosing the wrong track for the train, I go off course. When I admit my weakness, affirm the work of the Cross, surrender to His will, and follow His way, His righteous life supplants the flesh and puts me on the track to triumph. Suddenly my own track, which loomed so close, has faded in the distance, and my eyes are again opened to see myself and others from His heavenly perspective.

Righteousness then radiates outward, not in duties or rituals, but through the motivating force of God's own character in me. Now it becomes natural to consider the welfare of another above personal comfort.

Imagine the protection, the strength, the triumph of such oneness. Standing together against the enemy, helping each other put on our royal clothes, interceding, encouraging, holding one another up, maintaining a clear vision of victory for one another. What a triumph!

❧ WEARING HIS WARDROBE ❧

You cannot wear righteousness as your covering unless you believe and receive the truths about your new identity in Christ. When you accept, appropriate, and affirm Christ's righteousness, He makes it a vibrant reality in your life. A marvelous transformation takes place from the inside out as you learn to think and express His truth about yourself.

Morning and evening, meditate on these affirmations of your identity in Christ. Write them on cards, carry them with you and review often during the day. Let them open your eyes to see yourself and others through His eyes of unconditional love and acceptance.

Isaiah 61:10-11
Galatians 2:20
Galatians 3:6

CHAPTER FOUR

CLOTHED WITH

❧ PREPARING FOR BATTLE ❧

Are you seeking an oasis—a peaceful resting place from the stress of modern life? Like a cool stream of mountain water in the heat and confusion of today's values and philosophies, true peace flows from our King to revive the wilting heart.

Many people outside and within the church yearn for escape from the feverish pace of today's world to the simpler path of peace. The way begins and ends with a personal relationship with the Prince of Peace Himself—Jesus Christ. Apart from Him, peace remains an optimistic illusion. While the world ignores the true source of peace, Jesus offers Himself as the answer to everyone who seeks Him: "Come to Me all who are weary and heavy-laden, and I will give you rest" (Matthew 11:28).

Precious Prince of Peace, I come to You for rest. Teach me Your truths, then cover me with peace. Keep me immovable in You no matter how hard the storms blow. Make me one with Your heart and purpose, so that my life may spread the message of Your perfect peace. Thank You.

Prayerfully review Psalm 23.
1. Which part(s) of this psalm brings you His peace today? Why?

2. What must a lamb do in order to rest peacefully with the Shepherd? See John 10:4, 27.

Review Ephesians 6:10-18.

3. How can you keep your "feet shod with the preparation of the Gospel of peace"?

4. Define peace both from the world's point of view and from God's perspective. What is the main difference?

5. Why is it so important to be "girded with truth" and to wear "the breastplate of righteousness" before we can know and live in His peace?

6. All the following verses contain the promise of God's peace. What condition do you see in each for realizing that peace?

Isaiah 26:3

John 14:27

John 16:33

Romans 5:1-2

Philippians 4:4-7

7. Which of the above Scriptures affirm the fact that you already have been given His peace?

Study Ephesians 2:13-22.
8. Paraphrase and personalize verses 13 and 14.

9. What had to take place so that you would have peace?

10. Define the word *reconcile* (v. 16).

11. Describe Jesus as you see Him in verses 17-18.

12. Look at your identity in verses 19-22. Enjoy it! Count on it! Who are you?

13. Second Corinthians 5:17-20 gives further insight into the wonderful meaning of reconciliation. Because Jesus reconciled you to Himself, you are a _____ (v. 17) and an _____ (v. 20). Since you are one with Him, what ministry do you share with Him?

Read Isaiah 52:7.
14. Having your feet shod with the Gospel of peace brings responsibility along with the blessing of personal peace. What message is God speaking to you here?

15. You cannot bring peace unless you are wearing peace as part of your armor. Did you lose your peace any time this week by neglecting other parts of the armor?

16. Pray the words of the hymn "Jesus, I Am Resting, Resting." If you believe and affirm its message with all your heart, you are putting on His armor and you are being filled with His peace. Write a prayer of thanks for His gift.

🐚 PUTTING ON HIS WORD 🐚

One day, years ago, when I felt anything but peace, I discovered a little verse in an old hymnal. Suddenly my mind grasped a fantastic truth, and my broken spirit began to soar. "I live in the heavenlies with Jesus," my heart sang. "Nothing can disturb me here."

The comfort of this truth has never left me. Often, in the rush of the day, I remind myself that the real me is "far above" with my King. When by faith, I put on peace, He transports my soul to His high places where I view the world and its circumstances from His perspective of quiet triumph. Nothing can touch me there.

The Prince of Peace. Spiritual warfare is a constant reality. Yet peace is ours as citizens of His kingdom, for His life is our shelter. As long as I stand firm in my Prince, peace reigns. But when I shift my focus from Him to my wants and circumstances (including my own desire for peace), anxiety, guilt, fear, resentment, and confusion creep in. Quietly my Prince reminds me, "Be still and know that I am God." In a moment, my eyes are back on Him, He fills His place in the center of my heart, and peace again reigns.

In order to stand firm, I must remember that the Prince of Peace is also Truth and Righteousness to me.

First, I affirm the truth of His greatness and my own need. He is the mighty sovereign God who wisely and lovingly cares for me. He is my Warrior, my Strength, my Wisdom, and my Love. Nothing is impossible for Him.

Next, I remember that the Prince of Peace is my righteousness. Not by my effort, but by His death and resurrection life, I stand pure and holy before my God. Satan cannot disturb me with his accusations and lies when Jesus, my righteousness, covers me.

Coming to Him. Mary and Martha both loved Jesus. One sister drew near to Him; the other, concerned about her circumstances, became anxious and lost her peace. To her, Jesus spoke a very special message:

Martha, Martha, you are worried and bothered about so many things; but only a few things are necessary, really only one, for Mary has chosen the good part, which shall not be taken away from her. (Luke 10:41-42)

Resting at the feet of Jesus—this is the life of peace. Its single focus—God! Its one desire—to know, please, and honor Him. Its solitary pursuit—to walk with Him in His purpose. All else is secondary.

Steps to peace. Jesus took the first step for me. Through the cross, He "broke down the barrier" between His holy character and my sinful nature (Ephesians 2:12-22).

The next step is mine. I believed and received Him who is my Peace. Now, when I choose to put on His garments, the Prince of Peace covers me, and I am filled with His peace.

The same four choices that produce a lifestyle of truth and righteousness also bring the peace that triumphs over any earthly disturbance: *feeding on the peace in His Word; meditating on truths that promote peace; filtering for truths about peace; following His lifestyle of peace.*

Finally, God calls me to share His work. With the privilege of enjoying His peace comes the responsibility of a peacemaker. But before I go, I must *seek* Him and *listen* to His voice. My seeking and listening continue while I work, if not by conscious thought, by an inner attitude of attentive submission to the will of God.

Any resistance to His voice or will stirs up strife and leaves me powerless against my enemies. On the other hand, when I surrender to the Prince of Peace, He fills me with His life and gives me His love-filled peace of reconciliation and rest to share with everyone in my path.

Peace with each other. While peace (*eirene*) refers to the inner tranquility which flows from oneness with the King, it also means harmony and concord with others. He desires our cooperation to make this bond of peace a living, practical reality among us.

Consider these facts:

☐ Through God's unconditional love in you, others can experience their total acceptance in Christ. He offers forgiveness, worth, a caring community, a new life.

☐ The most persuasive proof of His accepting love is unspoken—your love and appreciation for each person, your availability, your willingness to listen and participate in another's life. When you do speak words that affirm someone's worth in Christ, be sure your action matches your words.

☐ Differences should build unity and interdependence, not disharmony. Each of us, with our own pattern of strengths, weaknesses, and temperaments, carries a special fragrance of the life of Jesus. Thus we fit into each other's lives and complete the body of Jesus.

The way of a peacemaker. Jesus calls me to follow Him, to live, walk, love, and restore as He did, and to guard my heart against any hindrance to His work in and through me. Most people in my own neighborhood remain separated from Him. They are my mission field.

Jesus' ministry of reconciliation is a simple, but not a soft, way of life. It calls me to love sacrificially, lay down my life, share the suffering of others, bear their burdens, and witness the triumph of truth whether or not people will believe.

We are adequate—in Him! I must choose to depend on Him for everything—wisdom, guidance, provision, and strength. When He directs, I must follow. If I deviate from the path of faith to follow the way of self-effort, I lose my peace.

Jesus never strayed from His Father's direction and strength. He had learned, as we must, that He could "do nothing of Himself, unless it is something He sees the Father doing" (John 5:19).

His Father's work brought Him to the end of self's resources. Likewise, my Father's work for me will gradually produce freedom from self in me. Then, as that death nears completion, I will know increasing peace and surrender in His will. For the lifeless corpse of self cannot complain, argue, disobey, or run away.

Peace reigns when I am yoked to Jesus. When the path of peace becomes steep and rocky, He points my heart to the joy that lies ahead. When storm clouds threaten, He reminds me that the sunlight of His love never dims. As I behold my King, see His purpose, and receive the peace and power of His life, He transforms the weary climb into sweet fellowship with Himself, and the pressing tumult into peaceful rest in His arms.

Unconditional peace. Jesus knows how easily I forget my heavenly citizenship, focus on circumstances, and lose my peace. Therefore, He reminds me to take and wear *His* peace which never changes:

> Peace I leave with you; My peace I give to you; not as the
> world gives, do I give to you. Let not your heart be troubled,
> nor let it be fearful. (John 14:27)

Long ago a man sought the perfect picture of peace. Not finding one that satisfied, he announced a contest to produce this masterpiece. The challenge stirred the imagination of artists everywhere, and paintings arrived from far and wide. Finally the great day of revelation arrived.

The judges uncovered one peaceful scene after another, while the viewers clapped and cheered.

The tensions grew. Only two pictures remained veiled. As a judge pulled the cover from one, a hush fell over the crowd. A mirror-smooth lake reflected lacy, green birches under the soft blush of the evening sky. Along the grassy shore, a flock of sheep grazed undisturbed. Surely this was the winner.

The man with the vision uncovered the second painting himself, and the crowd gasped in surprise. Could this be peace? A tumultuous waterfall cascaded down a rocky precipice; the crowd could almost feel its cold, penetrating spray. Stormy-grey clouds threatened to explode with lightning, wind and rain. In the midst of the thundering noises and bitter chill, a spindly tree clung to the rocks at the edge of the falls. One of its branches reached out in front of the torrential waters as if foolishly seeking to experience its full power.

A little bird had built a nest in the elbow of that branch. Content and undisturbed in her stormy surroundings, she rested on her eggs. With her eyes closed and her wings ready to cover her little ones, she manifested peace that transcends all earthly turmoil.

Put on the Prince of Peace and enjoy His stillness through every storm in *your* life.

❧ WEARING HIS WARDROBE ❧

To experience peace we must transfer the focus of our heart *from* the people, pace, and pressures around us *to* the presence of our King. His Word facilitates both the choice and the change. You don't have to read long passages. A few verses made alive in your heart may be your catalyst to peace year after year. Psalm 23 continues to bring this comfort to me. Try working through its verses, then repeating the journey every day this week. If you follow these steps, you will find each day's meditation richer than the one before.

1. Review chapter 2 of this book.

2. Find a quiet place where you can meet your Shepherd. Be ready to receive whatever He wants to give you.

3. Pray with the psalmist, "Open my eyes, that I may behold wonderful things from Thy law" (Psalm 119:18).

4. Slowly read the first verse of Psalm 23, taking time to meditate on every thought and picture. Who is your Shepherd? How does He care for you? What does it mean to be His sheep?

5. David "saw" his beloved Shepherd. Let him share his vision with you. Biblical visualization is allowing the Holy Spirit to make the illustrations of the Word bright and vibrant in your mind's eye.

6. Having received His word, pray back the words from your own heart. As you give back what He has given, His gifts become more fully yours, because by them you are more deeply joined to Him.

7. Go on to the remaining verses, letting the Shepherd lead you through the pastures, the valleys, and the joys of communion with Him. When you have finished, carry the memories of your journey with you to keep His peace throughout the day.

CHAPTER FIVE

CLOTHED WITH

PREPARING FOR BATTLE

My faith rests in the one sovereign God who guides the whole vast universe, personally cares for me, and has the power to accomplish His very best in my life forever.

How, then, does faith become a power that works for me? As God's ambassador in this world, I live on a battlefield. Poisonous darts of discouragement, doubt, and despair bombard my mind and emotions. Without God's shield, they reach their mark.

Precious Lord, train me to take and carry Your faith as a shield every day. For when I forget, I am bombarded with thoughts and temptations that ignore or deny Your greatness, sovereignty, wisdom, and love. Teach me to be still and know that You are God.

Review the armor in Ephesians 6:13-17. Ask God for special insight into verse 16.

1. What promise do you see in verse 16?

What must you do to obtain the promise?

2. Why must you wear the preceding parts of the armor before you can hold up the shield of faith?

3. Define *faith*. See Hebrews 11:1 and a dictionary.

4. Describe any of your recent thoughts or actions which expressed the opposite of faith. What effect did these have on you and possibly others?

Read Matthew 14:24-33. The disciples experienced some very human reactions to their circumstance. Can you identify with them? As you answer the following questions, relate each to your own life.

5. What caused fear in the disciples? What has dismayed or frightened you recently?

6. What comforting words did Jesus speak? Hear Him say this to you.

7. Describe the expression of Peter's faith (vv. 28-29).

8. Genuine faith is expressed in positive choices. Describe a choice you made in genuine faith this week.

9. Why did Peter begin to sink? Why might you begin to sink?

10. Compare the rescue described here with the way Jesus, your Shepherd, lifts you up after a defeat.

Review the message of Galatians 2:20.
11. What comfort do you find in those words?

12. Ask God to speak to you about the life of Jesus. Then describe the faith of the Son of God—the faith which now is in you.

Read 2 Chronicles 14:11.
13. All of us are involved in some form of personal battle every day. Whether it is a painful "impossible" circumstance or simply a matter of disciplined choice-making, God offers victory. Pray with King Asa the words of 2 Chronicles 14:11 and expect God to act on your behalf.

14. Who does Asa recognize to be the participants in the battle? Who do these antagonists represent to you?

15. In the second half of his prayer, what four steps of action does King Asa take?

Of what is Asa confident?

Read 2 Chronicles 16:1-3, 7-9. After his victory, Asa became self-confident and fought a different kind of battle.
16. Where did Asa turn for strength this time?

What were the consequences of putting his faith in man rather than God?

17. What have you learned from Asa's example? Can you identify with his failure or his victory?

Read 2 Chronicles 20:12.
18. As you face the "great multitude who are coming against" you, as Jehoshaphat did, what must you recognize about yourself and choose to do?

19. Paraphrase and personalize 1 John 4:4 and 5:4. Keep these verses hidden in your heart. They are great swords in battle.

20. In the next few days, be ready to fight and win even in the smallest conflicts of your life. A small battle is training ground for bigger battles. Describe one of these battles. How did you take up the shield of faith?

❧ PUTTING ON HIS WORD ❧

Caught in the unyielding crawl of five-o'clock freeway traffic one evening, I cried out to God for peace, patience, and relief from inner pressure. There was nothing else to do other than worry, complain, and churn inside. Immediately the Spirit reminded me of God's perspective:

> Consider it all joy, my brethren, when you encounter various trials, knowing that the testing of your faith produces endurance. And let endurance have its perfect result, that you may be perfect and complete, lacking in nothing. (James 1:2-3)

I laughed and the tension faded. I remembered times when a phone call or an unexpected visitor delayed my leaving for an appointment while, at the other end, God adjusted (usually by some sort of delay) the other person's timetable. My King reigns! His program aims primarily, not to fulfill *my* plans for the day, but to transform me into His likeness through the exercise of faith.

Faith has one object: God. I trust not in what I have seen and experienced, but in my sovereign King for Whom nothing is impossible.

Faith is an intimate personal relationship with Jesus, my King. I don't need to know *where* I am going, *what* tomorrow will bring, or *why* something happens. I just need to know the One *Who* is my Shepherd.

Faith opens my heart to receive and enjoy all God's resources.

Faith motivates me to action. It compels me to participate in the fulfillment of its own vision.

Faith releases power. It makes truth effective in and through me.

Faith has an eternal perspective. It looks beyond today's struggles and tomorrow's schedule to God's eternal purpose. It pierces through the limitations of sense, sight, and the temporary material world and opens the door to true and lasting reality.

The world says that "seeing is believing" or "I'll believe it when I see it." God says that *"believing* is seeing" and "You will see it when you *believe* it." Many years ago, Elisha and his servant watched the mighty Syrian army approach their shelter. The servant trembled with fear, but God's faithful prophet stood firm and confident on God's promise of protection: "Do not fear, for those who are with us are more than those who are with them" (2 Kings 6:16). Turning to God, the prophet prayed and the Lord revealed the horses and chariots of fire to his servant.

Fortunately, God seldom provides sight into the unseen to help us believe. If He did, we would need no faith and receive no reward. Remember Jesus' encouragement, "Blessed are they who did not see, and yet believed" (John 20:29).

When faith assures me that God in His eternal wisdom has planned each day of my life, I walk forward with confidence and anticipation. When Jesus and His invisible kingdom become more real to me, the peace of God's presence reigns in me. Out of this faith grows a spiritual alertness.

The power of faith. Through faith, the power of my King is released into me to accomplish His purpose. Look at these examples of active faith:

☐ God warned Noah about things he could not possibly see or understand, things so incredible that others ridiculed and rejected Him. Noah's faith enabled him to stand alone with his family against the pressures of the world as He carried out a heavenly assignment which made no earthly sense.

☐ Abraham's faith motivated and enabled him to leave home, travel to a distant land, live as a migrant, receive and relinquish his precious son, and keep his heart focused on a heavenly kingdom. Faith brought the continual assurance that every sacrifice was well worth the reward of eternal friendship with God.

☐ By faith Moses knew that disgrace for the sake of his God was of greater value than the treasures in Egypt. Therefore, he chose to be mistreated along with the people of God rather than to enjoy the pleasures of sin for a short time.

Genuine faith is born in humility and need, grows by the Word and obedience, and is tested in the crucible of suffering. It produces peace, patience, and perseverance as it looks forward to eternal union with Jesus. What a victory!

Will I step out in reckless, confident faith when He calls me away from the familiar?

The triumph of faith. The same paragraph in Hebrews 11 that lists the great feats of faith concludes with an equally awesome account of terrible earthly tragedies that became fantastic heavenly victories:

> Others were tortured, not accepting their release, in order that they might obtain a better resurrection; and others experienced mockings and scourgings, yes, also chains and imprisonment. They were stoned, they were sawn in two, they were tempted, they were put to death with the sword. (Hebrews 11:35-37)

Which is the greater triumph—faith to live or faith to die? Which brings my heart closer to Jesus?

Paul's faith focused on the unseen, eternal riches of oneness with Jesus. He could rejoice in the midst of suffering, for he knew that from human weakness and pain would flow eternal triumph and glory.

Consistent faith-life demonstrates God's triumph by trusting when nothing makes sense, thanking when everything hurts, and walking when I feel like fainting. It guards against fear, hopelessness, anger—feelings that often spring from the lack of eternal vision and purpose. It builds in me the character of Jesus.

Faith follows Jesus. Do you believe you are being watched? Have you fixed your hope on the "joy ahead"? Do these realities motivate you to faithfully live the message of God's unconditional, reconciling love before the unseen viewers?

When my faith remains fixed on Jesus and His purpose, I receive the needed power to love as He did. Useless is the wavering belief that draws no power to follow. The faith that follows Jesus begins with accepting all that God tells me about His unconditional love and grace for me. I am a new creation, precious and beautiful in His sight, worthy to enter His presence, equipped to conquer every enemy, mighty to win the battles of the kingdom.

Next, it carries the same message of love and victory to others. For through the eyes of faith, I see each person—my husband, children, friends, salespersons, bankers—as precious, loved, worthy, and needy.

The faith of Jesus. Have you ever felt crushed rather than comforted by wonderful promises such as, "With God all things are possible"? (Matthew 19:26) I have. Aware of my own failing faith, I have cried out like the man who came to Jesus, "I do believe; help my unbelief" (Mark 9:21). Then Jesus helped me to see that it was the power of *His* faith, not my own, that brought victory. When I take the shield of faith, I appropriate the life of my King, including His mighty faith.

Taking the shield. How do I appropriate the faith of Jesus Christ? Will I think, believe, and act according to the way of faith or the way of the flesh? If I forget to choose, I run the way of the flesh which will lead to disappointments, frustration, hopelessness, and despair. To choose faith, I must consciously choose the path that leads to peace, hope, and victory.

I can choose the way of faith by whispering a few simple words to my King: "Jesus, I am yours. Please take over." "Jesus, I need you. Reign in me." "Jesus, I love you." Any words that express my conscious choice to surrender will fill and cover me with the faith of my King.

This simple action, of course, is built on God's Word. I have already filled my mind with the truths of God's character, purpose, and love-relationship with me. I have accepted His righteousness, and I am trusting Him to nudge me whenever I forget to take "every thought captive to the obedience of Christ" (2 Corinthians 10:5).

When I remind myself of past triumphs, Christ's life flows into me, and faith grows to match the present challenge. On days when faith burns dimly and my memory bank brings up failures rather than spiritual feats, I read my praise journal, a diary of thanks to my King for specific miracles and love-touches. Its reminders of past delights with Jesus fan the flame of faith and bring me back on the track of triumph.

God's school of faith includes tests which consistently reveal the track I have chosen—self or God. Self will complain, despair, and give up. But when I follow God, I remember to speak words of faith. Immediately my heart sees beyond the visible circumstances to the Heavenly King whose purpose for this moment is far higher than my human sense can perceive. Before an invisible host, I have the opportunity to glorify God through my simple response of faith. Each time I "keep the faith" throughout the test, I take a step closer to the triumphant faith-life of constant peace, surrender, and communion with my King.

❦ *WEARING HIS WARDROBE* ❦

Learn to listen to your own thoughts. You are not responsible for every thought that comes to your mind, but for handling each one according to truth. Satan and your flesh may seed thoughts to your mind, but you can reject the ones that contradict God. Then, when you claim truth and act on it, you manifest faith.

Writing in your journal each day this week will help you become aware of your thought patterns and more sensitive to their effects. Ask God to help you hear and discern your own thoughts, then record:

☐ Thoughts and consequent actions that manifest unbelief.

☐ Thoughts and actions that manifest faith.

☐ The subsequent victory.

Finally, lift up the shield of faith by writing God a love-letter telling Him who He is to you. Give Him thanks.

CHAPTER SIX

CLOTHED WITH *Salvation*

⚜ PREPARING FOR BATTLE ⚜

Salvation has three parts: past, present, and future. In a special moment of time, when I received Jesus Christ as my Saviour, I was born into His kingdom. This step has become history; it remains an accomplished fact whether or not I choose to wear the helmet of salvation.

At the cross, Jesus also won for me continual saving grace which enables me to "reign" with Him today and forever (Romans 5:17). This part of my salvation depends on my daily choice to wear the whole armor. Then, dressed in the King's clothes, I can look forward to unbroken fellowship and communion with Him for all eternity.

The *final salvation* occurs when Jesus Himself returns to receive me as His bride. In the bright light of His countenance, I will be changed in the twinkling of an eye. What a day that will be when I will be like Him!

Precious King, show me how to wear Your salvation—the durable covering of Your own precious life. Then make me an extension of Your saving power to others. Let nothing destroy the joy and peace of Your victory nor mar the image of Your triumphant life in me. Thank You.

Read Ephesians 6:17.
1. What does God remind you to do?

Read Ephesians 1:18-23. This beautiful prayer shows God's authority and power to keep you safe in Him every moment of your life here on earth.
2. As you pray these words with Paul, notice the three heavenly resources available to you. What is God showing you about each?

Look at Ephesians 2:6.
  3. When Jesus initially saved you, what did He do for you?

    How does this divine action keep you safe in Him today?

Read 1 Thessalonians 5:8-11. This passage will give you a deeper understanding of God's message in Ephesians 6:17.
  4. What does the helmet represent?

  5. Paul encourages you to "be alert and sober" (1 Thessalonians 5:6). What does this mean to you in the context of this passage?

  6. In verse 10, what does God promise you? Why is this significant?

  7. Define *hope* and explain how Biblical hope differs from the world's hope.

Read Romans 8:16-25. Paul counted on God's salvation for each day. Yet, during his lifetime, he waited expectantly for something infinitely greater.
  8. Describe the hope Paul expressed ın verses 18-23?

  9. What do you learn about hope in verses 24-25?

Read Romans 13:10-14. Notice how the approaching time of salvation motivates Paul to action.

10. Do God's words through Paul encourage you? Why or why not?

11. Hope is an essential choice for those who would live a life of victory. What do the following exhortations tell you about hope?

Hebrews 6:11-15

Hebrews 6:18-19

Hebrews 10:23

Read Hebrews 11:8-10. Notice the motivating force in Abraham which caused him to obey God and follow Him no matter what the cost.

12. What did Abraham seek? Can you identify with him? In what ways?

Read 1 Peter 1:3-13. Look at the joy and praise of Peter's heart as he remembered all the magnificent heavenly treasures awaiting him.

13. What does "living hope" mean to you? (v. 3)

14. Describe *your* inheritance (v. 4).

15. Write the beautiful promise in verse 5, making it your own. Which stage(s) of salvation do you see here?

16. In the light of God's eternal perspective, what is your attitude toward the present trials in your life? (vv. 6-7)

17. What does the "helmet of the hope of salvation" protect you against? Explain.

How do you "put on" and wear the helmet of salvation? (v. 13)

Read 1 John 3:1-3.
18. Summarize the exhortation and promise given here?

19. Write a "thank-You note" to your King for all that He has given you in the helmet of salvation.

❧ *PUTTING ON HIS WORD* ❧

Jesus *saved* me the moment I believed and received Him. He *saves* me daily as I trust and follow Him. He *will save* me from the final traces of earthly pain and imperfections on that great day when I meet Him face-to-face.

By faith, I receive both past and present salvation, undeserved gifts bought with His blood. Any attempt to earn His approval or pay Him back insults the Giver, whose gift is worth far more than anything I could ever offer.

Can a child pay her parents for their love and care? Would a father want payment? No, for love delights to give. Our Father gladly shares His riches, asking only that the gift be received and treasured. The response He seeks is not pay or performance but worship and obedience.

Daily salvation. With each day's challenge, I face a choice: Will I live and walk by sight and self or by faith and Spirit? My answer comes from deep within:

> As for me, I shall call upon God, and the Lord will save me. Evening and morning and at noon, I will complain and murmur, and He will hear my voice. He will redeem my soul in peace from the battle which is against me, for they are many who strive with me. (Psalm 55:16-18)
>
> God is my salvation, I will trust and not be afraid. (Isaiah 12:2)
>
> I will lift up my eyes to the mountains; from whence shall my help come? My help comes from the Lord Who made heaven and earth. (Psalm 121:1-2)

I know that "my flesh and my heart may fail, but God is the strength of my heart and my portion forever" (Psalm 73:26). Therefore, I yield my finite life and futile efforts to Him, trusting Him to take over and win the battle. He asks only that I trust Him, wear my helmet, and cooperate with His plan for victory.

How do I do this? I put on the helmet of salvation when I affirm and apply the promises of His strength, sufficiency, and sovereignty. Whatever the conflict, He has provided a truth that fits and wins. Do I fear? He assures me of His power and availability. Am I tempted to worry? He reminds me of His kind wisdom and eternal plan. Too little time? My time is in His hands.

When my heart is slow to absorb these truths, I speak them out loud. Sometimes I hear the spoken word more clearly than my silent thoughts. When "I confess with my mouth" the saving truths stored in my mind, the enemy loosens his grip and the battle abates.

Power to save. When you and I wear His salvation, Jesus not only keeps us safe, He also makes us living extensions of His saving life to others. He has given us authority and power to make His eternal triumphs effective in our everyday lives. Listen to Jesus' words: "I will give you the keys of the kingdom of heaven; whatever you bind on earth will be bound in heaven, and whatever you loose on earth will be loosed in heaven" (Matt. 16:19). Covered with His garments of salvation we may wield His authority over all hindrances. We may release His peace and freedom to those held captive to fear, anger, hopelessness, and futility.

Just as eternal salvation becomes effective only when we believe and receive Jesus, so this daily salvation requires our faith and appropriation. We must believe in His heavenly victories, apply them to our lives today, then watch salvation become an ongoing, transforming force.

This Spirit-directed power is strictly limited to what He has already accomplished at the cross. Look at these marvelous triumphs that show what we can claim for ourselves and extend to one another:

☐ At the cross, Jesus put Satan in submission under His feet; disarmed the rulers and authorities of Satan; rendered Satan powerless; cast out the ruler of this world; threw down the accuser of the brethren and bound him. In reality, Satan is already defeated; so when we call his bluff and proclaim God's already accomplished victory, he must flee.

☐ On the cross, Jesus bore our sickness; became the guilt offering for all our sins—past, present and future; offered total forgiveness; freed us from our selfish sin nature; released us into a life of peace, wholeness, and love.

No longer need anyone be held captive to destructive guilt, habits, cravings, thoughts, and feelings. Our King has commissioned us to make His spiritual triumphs effective in our circumstances today.

Freed from bondage. Not long ago, a young woman named Ann asked me to pray that her intimacy with Jesus be restored. A few questions a weight of guilt. Although the young woman could give mental assent to Christ's atonement, her offenses seemed too great to be so readily forgiven. Something was blocking the restorative power of God's Word.

We prayed for insight, and God showed us that a temporary involvement in a Hindu cult had opened the door to Satanic oppression. His strongholds had to be torn down and her mind unveiled—a spiritual battle which implicates every part of the armor.

We began by proclaiming the truths of Christ's victories on the cross and applying them to Ann. We declared Satan a defeated foe, having no power over or access to Ann. In the name of our Lord Jesus Christ, we commanded Satan's forces of unbelief, deception, idolatry, and self-condemnation to leave her. We then tore down any strongholds raised against the knowledge of God, His character, and His power to forgive and cleanse. We released God's freedom, righteousness, love, and peace into Ann and thanked God.

Now Ann could freely receive God's life. As she read aloud about God's forgiveness in Luke 15:11-24, she sobbed. God was cleansing and restoring her soul by the "washing of water with the Word" (Ephesians 5:26). When Ann lifted her head, her eyes sparkled with the joy of God's presence, and her heart was filled with praise and thanks for God's marvelous victory.

Authority in Him. By God's authority, Ann was set free to receive God's riches. This same authority is available to all God's people when they wear His armor. To His people who are willing to share His death and resurrection life, Jesus offers authority to release the powers of the kingdom. Joined to Him in heart, life, and purpose, we may apply the realities of Christ's spiritual victories to our own needs and battles.

At the same time, we cannot refuse the sword of the Word and the cutting of the cross which releases us from the flesh. Saving power only flows from willing surrender to the dying process that releases His resurrection life.

Jesus walked and lived in total oneness with the heart and will of His Father. He only did what He saw the Father doing. Likewise, I can wield heavenly authority and power only according to the direction of my King. He alone knows the perfect time and place for loosing and binding, for training in endurance, and for release from a trial.

The triumph of hope. God's hope opens my ears to hear His direction and my heart to trust His timing. In the Old Testament, hope is referred to as *waiting on God*—patient, confident expectation that God will indeed accomplish all that He has promised.

My hope of salvation has prepared me to live in the full saving power of the kingdom. It has protected me against discouragement, futility, and despair. No matter how dark my day, I can count on bright light ahead.

My hope of salvation is for today. Like a pilot guiding his plane by radar through the night, so my Shepherd leads me through present temptation, danger, and darkness by His all-knowing wisdom, power, and love.

My hope of salvation is for tomorrow. No matter how difficult or painful my circumstances may be, I have a future more wonderful than anything imaginable. While I "wait on Him," Christ frees me from all forms of corruption. One day, He will present me as a holy and beautiful bride for all eternity.

The helmet of the hope of salvation sets our minds on the things above (Colossians 3:2). Therefore, like blinders on a horse, it guards us from distractions that would draw us off His course and away from the protection of His armor. While it keeps our eyes focused on our King, it transforms us into the likeness of the One we behold. In Him we are safe.

❧ *WEARING HIS WARDROBE* ❧

You put on the helmet of salvation when you affirm and apply the saving promises of God's strength, sufficiency, and sovereignty to your present circumstances. Follow these four steps each day.

1. As David treasured the memories of God's past triumphs (See Psalm 103), you also will be encouraged by reviewing God's victories in *your* life. Begin your day by remembering His personal love and care. What did He accomplish for you last year? Last week? Yesterday? Praise Him for His saving power.

2. Ask God to alert you to potential battles. What challenges do you face today? What enemy is stalking you? What weakness has brought recurrent defeat and discouragement in the past? Tell God your need. Ask Him for a Scripture that will assure you of His sufficiency and salvation in your circumstance. Meditate on the Scriptures below:

> 1 Thessalonians 5:8-11
> Isaiah 43:1-4
> Psalm 25:1, 4-5, or 16-21
> Psalm 60:10-12
> Psalm 61:1-4
> Psalm 62:1-2
> Psalm 63:7-8

3. Write God a love letter describing your victory. He already knows, but He loves to listen to your heart speaking to Him and giving Him thanks. These documented triumphs will continue to bring encouragement in future battles.

4. Some of your victories may be private, while others have power to build faith and hope in people around you. Tell someone what God is doing for you. Your testimony will enlarge your faith and encourage your friend to trust God as you do.

CHAPTER SEVEN

CLOTHED WITH THE

Word

❧ *PREPARING FOR BATTLE* ❧

Temptations crowd into my life daily, and I long for a way to silence thoughts filled with doubt, lies, and accusations. Fortunately, God has given me a marvelous weapon, certain to win the battle no matter how strong the enemy—the Word of God. It is the one part of God's armor which is primarily offensive rather than defensive. And, when properly handled, it is guaranteed to send the enemy on a fast retreat.

God tells me to "take the sword" which He has given me. Held and wielded by faith, it cuts through all bondages and destroys every enemy stronghold. My King is the living Word, my Sword! He joined me to Himself, so that my arm raised in battle is, in fact, His arm raised in triumph over all the forces of the enemy.

Daily I will seek Him, dress in the "full armor of God," then go out ready and equipped to win. When I encounter obstacles to the peace and freedom He has promised, His sword in my hand will cut them down and bring victory in His name.

Jesus, precious Word of God, teach me to wield Your powerful sword as You did. Against every tempting lie, You raised that standard of the Word and triumphed. Which Scripture shall be my sword in each of my battles today? Show me, so that Your purpose be fulfilled through my life today. Thank You, my King.

Read Psalm 91. Make each verse your own. Listen and hear how much He loves you.

1. In which verses does God show you the whole armor or its parts?

V:4 with his pinnons he will cover you
his faithfulness is a buckler & a shield

Read Jesus' prayer for you in John 17:13-23.

2. According to verse 13, what does God long to see in you? How has

Joy

God prepared and equipped you to live out His life and victory in this world? See verses 14, 17, 21-23 and relate these to the armor.

I gave them your word — Your word is Truth.

3. Describe the link between the sword and the Word of God in each of the following:

Ephesians 6:17

And take the helmet of salvation and the sword of the Spirit, which is the word of God.

Hebrews 4:12

The word of God is living & effective, sharper than any two-edged sword penetrating even between soul and spirit, joints & marrow & able to discern reflections & thoughts.

Revelation 19:11-16

name inscribed that no one knows except Himself Cloak — & his name was called the Word of God

+ Out of his mouth a sharp sword to strike the nations.

4. Why is it possible for you to claim and use the authority and power of these swords?

The swords are the word of God.

Read Luke 4:1-13.

5. What special event occurred just before the tempter approached Jesus? *fasting 40 days & nights*

6. Do you see in Jesus' experience a pattern for a sequence that sometimes takes place in your own life? Explain.

7. List Jesus' three areas of temptation and relate each to a corresponding battle in your own life.

food —

power —

tempt God —

8. How does Satan use God's Word? Remember that he is called "an angel of light" (2 Corinthians 11:14) who knows and believes the truth but refuses to follow (James 2:19).

And no wonder for even Satan masquerades as an angel of light. You believe that God is one -- Even the demons believe that & tremble.

In light of Satan's use of Scriptures for his evil purposes, why is it essential that we know the Word of God?

9. Satan engaged Jesus in a spiritual war. How did Jesus win each battle?

By quoting scripture

10. In verse 13, what do you learn about Satan and his strategies?

Read 2 Corinthians 10:3-6.

11. Describe the power of your weapon, the sword of the Spirit.

enormously powerful, capable of destroying fortresses raise arguments vs knowledge of God thought captive in obedience to R - punish disobedience

12. Recall a battle you have fought recently "according to the flesh." Compare it with a battle you chose to fight God's way.

13. List the battlefields in your life and ask God to give you at least one sword from His Word for each area of battle.

Read Nehemiah 4. God's work of rebuilding the wall around Jerusalem after the Babylonian captivity progressed under Nehemiah's leadership. Their enemies made repeated attempts to hinder the completion of God's work just as Satan and his forces try to stop God's work today. Consider how each of the following questions relates to *your* warfare and victory.

14. Describe the attack of the enemy in Nehemiah 4. What was their strategy and intent? *plotted - surprise attack*

15. Having lost the first round, the enemies prepared a new battle plan (vv. 7-8). Compare this plan with the strategy of Satan in his attempts to defeat you.

    Give the two-fold response of the people (v. 9).

    Then, what did the enemy do? (v. 11)

    What extensive plan of action was adopted in order to carry on God's work successfully? (vv. 13-23)
    Carried a sword

16. As God's family, how can we apply Nehemiah's plan to our work of building up one another into one mature body in Christ?

17. Share an instance when you helped a friend put on her armor piece by piece. How did you do it, and what specific sword did you suggest to her?

18. Thank God for being and providing all that you need to live triumphantly now and forever.

Eph. 6-17 and take the helmet of Salvation and the sword of the Spirit, which is the sword of God.

✦ PUTTING ON HIS WORD ✦

What temptations did you face this week? Which kinds of subtle suggestions broke down your resistance? You probably bypassed the big, obvious ones without hesitation, but how did you handle the marginal proposals of self-pity, resentment, and anxiety.

Perhaps you struggle with overindulgence. When you walk by a bakery, the tantalizing fragrance of oven-fresh rolls traps your attention. You stop and gaze at the banquet of frosted, buttered delicacies. Among all the creamy pastries, a light, flaky croissant looks innocent enough—no sugar, no chocolate, mostly air. You are not all that hungry but, at the sight of this crusty delight, a silent cry for satisfaction rises from within.

Or perhaps the soft, blue sweater in the next window catches your imagination. What a perfect match with the blue skirt you bought on sale last week! How well it would underline your blue eyes. You could charge it for now, then cut down on something else.

An old friend walks by, and the next temptation finds an open door with the first casual question: "What's new?" Much has happened since last you talked. Before you know it, you are describing your latest spiritual, financial, and relational successes—"I shared Christ with my neighbor," or "My son got straight A's!" Wonderful! But who is getting the credit? Who is exalted?

The way to victory. Immediately after the great moment of affirmation at the Jordan River, the Spirit led Jesus into the wilderness. Then Jesus found Himself alone in the mountainous wilderness, hungry after fasting forty days, and vulnerable. Satan, always on the lookout for such opportunities, appeared.

In his most seductive voice, Satan whispered, "If You are the Son of God, command that these stones become bread" (Matthew 4:3). Jesus saw the deception and pulled out His sword: "It is written, 'Man shall not live on bread alone, but on every word that proceeds out of the mouth of God' " (v. 4). With a thrust of the Word, He won the spiritual battle in the physical arena.

But the devil had other tricks. Satan brought Jesus to the pinnacle of the temple and declared, "If You are the Son of God, throw Yourself down; for it is written, 'He will give His angels charge concerning You' " (v. 6).

In a moment Jesus could have demonstrated His heavenly status and authority to all the skeptics in the world, but instead He stood firm and wielded the sword of the Word against spiritual pride: "It is written, 'You shall not put the Lord your God to the test' " (v. 7). Jesus had no need to prove His identity, His authority, nor His Father's love. Trust in and obedience to the Word guaranteed that the far greater riches and triumph of the eternal Kingdom were His forever.

Finally, from a high mountain, Satan showed Jesus the kingdoms and riches of the world and made an offer: "All these things I will give You, if You fall down and worship me" (v. 9). Again Jesus responded with His sword, "Be gone, Satan! For it is written, 'You shall worship the Lord your God and serve Him only' " (v. 10). Never would He compromise the relationship, purpose, and identity He shared with His Father for the temporary emotional pleasure of worldly power and riches.

"But I'm not like Jesus," you might protest. "He was so pure, so close to His Father, so different from me. No wonder He resisted every temptation!"

Don't forget that our King stripped Himself of all personal power and glory, so that His life would demonstrate only what God can do through mere man:

> Therefore, He had to be made like His brethren in all things, that He might become a merciful and faithful high priest in things pertaining to God, to make propitiation for the sins of the people. (Hebrews 2:17)
> Let us therefore draw near with confidence to the throne of grace, that we may receive mercy and may find grace to help in time of need. (Hebrews 4:15-16)

Power of the Word. From the beginning of time, Jesus exercised the incredible power of His sword: "By the word of the Lord the heavens were made, and by the breath of His mouth all their host" (Psalm 33:6). The same power that created the world will one day judge it. Take a glimpse into the future: "He will strike the earth with the rod of His mouth, and with the breath of His lips He will slay the wicked" (Isaiah

11:4). Isaiah knew that he could exercise that power. Filled with the wonder of God's mighty presence, the prophet acknowledged, "He has made my mouth like a sharp sword; in the shadow of His hand He has concealed me" (Isaiah 49:2). Having heard his Lord, he could affirm God's will and walk in the same triumph God now offers us.

Notice the Word's effectiveness against both inner and outer foes:

> For the word of God is living and active and sharper than any two edged sword, and piercing as far as the division of soul and spirit, of both joints and marrow, and able to judge the thoughts and intentions of the heart. (Hebrews 4:12)

The power of the Word operates in two directions. First, it pierces through the soul, releasing discernment and truth. It breaks the tentacles of the temptation, focuses the mind on God, and purifies the intentions of the heart.

Second, it shows Satan that his door of opportunity in you has closed. By its piercing light, it forces him to flee. The true nature of the Word baffles our finite minds. Only by God's Spirit can we grasp, not only what the Word says, but also what it represents: the very life and power of our King before Whom all darkness disappears.

The key condition for releasing that power is faith—the kind of faith that takes, trusts, and follows. It is true that God's word will not return void, but if this promise proves that every word sown will bear fruit, *all* who hear it would follow Jesus.

Taking the Word. How, then, can I stand secure in the faith that releases the power of the Word in me? How do I "take" the sword of the Spirit and make it effective?

I start by making sure all the parts of the armor are secure. Unlike me who sometimes rushes into the battle spiritually naked, Jesus enters His battles fully dressed. Clothed in truth, righteousness, and peace with His Father, He can hold the shield of faith with confidence. Therefore, the power of the Word flows freely through His being.

We all have seen examples of wielding the Word without the armor. Remember the sharpness of a word spoken in judgment rather than love. Like any sharp instrument in unfit hands, the words may cut and slash an innocent victim, missing the real enemy entirely.

We maintain a condition of readiness by storing the written Word in our hearts and by making sure the armor is secured daily. When a crisis occurs, we take hold of the appropriate Word, and speak it against any lie or temptation Satan whispers into our thoughts. Then the power of the written Word flows from God into our hearts and wins the battle.

Transformed by the Word. My fiercest battles have occurred in the area of worth. I have always been very sensitive. Feelings of failure, rejection, and loneliness dig away at my fragile ego.

One day God showed me a verse that became my personal prayer and vision: "But I do not consider my life of any account as dear to myself, in order that I may finish my course" (Acts 20:24). I longed to be dead to my ego so that the vicissitudes of earthly relationships could no longer move or crush me.

When I pray for patience, God allows so many impatience-producing circumstances in my life that I can't possibly handle them myself. My inadequacy forces me to yield to God and take hold of His life in order to cope, then triumph.

The same kind of process brings death to self. Again and again I was forced, first to remember that I prayed to be made immovable in Him; and second, to count on His purpose and live. My personal point of view just emphasized the hurt and hopelessness, but the Word showed me about His eternal perspective:

> Unless a grain of wheat falls into the earth and dies, it remains by itself alone; but it if dies, it bears much fruit. He who loves his life loses it; and he who hates his life in this world shall keep it to life eternal. (John 12:24-25)

When I no longer count my self-life precious, nor hold on to it and try to save it by defending or pitying myself, I gain His eternal life—a life not moved to despair by circumstances or broken relationships.

The above Scriptures became my daily swords. As I took, trusted, and spoke them, they began to renew my mind and transform my thought patterns from the temporal to the eternal. The water of the Word's infinite insight was flushing out my own destructive view of self.

Another set of swords was needed to cancel out the thoughts of worthlessness sown by Satan. For a month I meditated morning and night on Scriptures that affirmed God's unending love for me: Psalm 139:1-18; Jeremiah 31:3; Romans 8:32-29; 1 John 3:1-3.

That month changed my life. No longer could Satan torment me with his demeaning taunts, "You don't fit; you'll only fail. They'll never like you." Through the power of the Word, I learned to see God's constant unconditional love over and above the fickle acceptance of people. I learned to walk with confidence through "impossible" circumstances. And I learned to discern and silence the lies that disturbed my peace. After all, I am one with the King of the universe! His Word in my mouth triumphs over every enemy. What more could I ask?

❦ WEARING HIS WARDROBE ❦

Every morning ask God to help you face the large and small battles of the day. Prepare yourself each morning with the following steps.

1. Put on the armor. Secure every part in its place, so that you are well covered by your King.

2. Review your supply of swords and make sure you take with you those you are most likely to need.

3. Trust that the swords you have chosen for the present conflict are your weapons, supplied and empowered by God to win the battles.

4. Speak your sword(s) against any lie, accusation, or temptation whispered into your thoughts by Satan.

5. In a prolonged battle, don't give up! Refuse to lay down your sword. Continue to fight to the finish. You may need to call a friend who can fight for and with you.

6. Write a note of thanks to your King for making His victory effective through His Word, your Sword.

7. Tell others what He has accomplished for you.

Jer. 31:3 With age-old love I have loved you; so I have kept my mercy toward you.

CHAPTER EIGHT

CLOTHED WITH

Praise

❧ *PREPARING FOR BATTLE* ❧

David offered praise in his victory and found victory in praise. Either one invites or follows the other.

When David spoke to God with words of praise, God filled David with His words of truth and power. Again and again David went out to battle with a heart that knew and praised God—then walked off the field a conqueror. It is no wonder that David's praise contained powerful affirmations of the truths of the whole armor of God.

David wore God's spiritual armor; therefore, he could lay aside the physical armor offered him for his battle against Goliath, the champion of the Philistines. After all, no giant can stand against Christ the King, our champion.

God, I praise You. Fill me with Your truth and power. Teach me how to wear Your armor so that I may become victorious over the Goliaths of my life. Thank You.

Read Psalm 18.

1. You can see that triumphant armor throughout Psalm 18. Some of the parts of the armor are clearly identified; others are only implied. Indicate the part of armor referred to along side the corresponding verse.

2. As you looked at God through David's eyes, what did He show you about Himself and His loving care for you?

Read 1 Samuel 17:26-50. Study the basis for David's great victory over Goliath. Again notice God's (not Saul's) armor for David. All the parts are included in this passage, including the garment of praise.
  3. Where do you find each piece of armor?

Read 2 Chronicles 20:1-22. The overwhelming military forces of Syria attacked God's people. Recognizing his desperate need, Jehoshaphat, king of Judah, turned to God in prayer and praise.
  4. Paraphrase verses 6 and 12.

  5. What did Jehoshaphat know about God?

     What did he know about himself?

  6. With what words did God reassure Jehoshaphat and his people? Store them in your heart and mind for your own battles.

  7. How did Jehoshaphat respond to God's encouragement? (v. 18)

  8. Describe Jehoshaphat's battle plan. How did God's people prepare for victory? What did God accomplish on their behalf?

9. Are you facing a difficult battle this week? How can you apply Jehoshaphat's strategy to your own circumstance?

Read Psalm 150.
10. Write the opening three words of this psalm.

These three words come from a single Hebrew word: *Hallelujah! Hallel* means praise; *Yah* refers to Yahweh, our Lord. What is God showing you about praise in this psalm?

11. Look up the word *praise* in a concordance. Count all the times God tells you to praise Him. What does this tell you about God's wise, loving concern for you?

12. Recall the truths God has shown you about Himself. Then write your own response to Him. *Praise* Him for all that He is to you. *Thank* Him for all that He has given and promised you. He loves to hear your words of praise and thanks because they open the door to your heart.

✄ *PUTTING ON HIS WORD* ✄

I didn't feel like praising God this morning, but I did open my Bible. I read the words David prayed the day Saul searched his house to kill him. Not only did David feel the stab of rejection, he now had to flee to the wilderness, leaving his home, wife, and best friend. Did he have reason to praise God? Listen:

> But as for me, I shall sing of Thy strength;
> Yes, I shall joyfully sing of Thy lovingkindness in the morning.
> For Thou hast been my stronghold,
> And a refuge in the day of my distress.
> O my strength, I will sing praises to Thee
> For God is my stronghold, the God who shows me loving-kindness. (Psalm 59:16-17)

Suddenly my momentary struggles seemed mild. In the light of David's praise, I saw my sovereign King and understood why He reminds me more than 180 times to praise Him. He longs to meet *my* need, not *His*. Praise turns my heart to God, produces worship, and prepares me to receive everything He longs to give me.

When I praise Him with my will, I affirm the truths He has deposited in my mind. The truths I think and speak in praise open my spiritual eyes to God's glory. Seeing Him, I worship Him; for praise builds an attitude of trust, adoration, humility, and surrender, which releases God's resources into my life.

The meaning of praise. Since praise is the prelude to worship and victory, I need to appreciate its nature and make it part of my life. The Old Testament word translated "praise" stems from three different Hebrew words:

1. *Shabah*—to soothe and still as well as to praise and commend. It is

usually an expression of praise to God for His mighty acts.

2. *Halal*—to praise, boast, rave, rejoice—boldly and often loudly. Today, whenever I sing "hallelujah" (*Halal* + *Yahweh*), I am summoning heavenly and earthly creatures to praise their Lord as did the seraphim in Isaiah 6.

Halal implies sincere, grateful, joyous appreciation for God and His great works—a praise which more often rose from the whole congregation than from a single person. It included choirs, musical instruments, singing, and dancing. Considered essential to formal public worship, halal praise must have been a time of joy, laughter, and wonderful fellowship with God and each other.

3. *Yadah*—to confess, praise, give thanks, or bring a thanksgiving offering. It usually expressed a person's public testimony of God's character, works, and active presence and help in his life.

Yadah praise naturally included thanks because, when I declare God's attributes and works, I plant thankfulness in my heart. Praise, therefore, produces an attitude of gratefulness and contentment.

The power of praise. Yadah praise played an impressive role in the history of God's people. Look back to the days of Jacob. Abraham's grandson bore 12 sons whose names still identify the tribes of Israel. When Leah, Jacob's unwanted wife, gave birth to their fourth son, she called him Judah, saying, "This time I will praise the Lord" (Genesis 29:35).

After four centuries of slavery in Egypt and a miraculous deliverance, God's people failed miserably in the wilderness—a consequence of their complaining attitude (the opposite of praise). For 40 years they attended God's school of faith, worship, love, and obedience where they learned to trust and love God. Then, on graduation day, they crossed the Jordan and entered the Promised Land. Led by praise, they triumphed and gained new territories as long as they remembered that sin blocks divine power. When they forgot God's lesson in obedience taught at Ai (Joshua 7), both praise and power crumbled.

Years later, praise won a dramatic victory through Jehoshaphat. God's faithful king trusted, obeyed, and acknowledged his utter weakness. Make Jehoshaphat's prayer your model for praise, faith, and humility:

> O Lord, the God of our fathers, art Thou not God in the heavens? And art Thou not ruler over all the kingdoms of the nations? Power and might are in Thy hand so that no one can stand against Thee. Didst Thou not, O our God, drive out the inhabitants of this land before Thy people

Israel, and give it to the descendants of Abraham Thy friend forever? O our God, wilt Thou not judge them? For we are powerless before this great multitude who are coming against us; nor do we know what to do, but our eyes are on Thee. (2 Chronicles 20:6-7, 12)

God responded with immediate assurance of victory. The next day, a team of worshipers led Jehoshaphat's army to the battlefield. Singing and praising God, they shouted, "Give thanks to the Lord, for His lovingkindness is everlasting" (2 Chronicles 20:21). While they sang and praised with uninhibited enthusiasm, God Himself ambushed their enemy and won the war (v. 22).

Praise produces purity. Praise brings double victory; it not only defeats the enemy, it purifies and prepares me for ever greater triumphs. When I praise God, His presence and character become increasingly real. As I "behold" His glory through the eyes of the Spirit, I am transformed! (2 Corinthians 3:18)

Just as praise purifies, so also complaint defiles. The Israelites in the wilderness complained to Moses about their treatment under God's protection. Their grumbling expressed lack of trust, ignorance of God's character, and an attitude of rebellion. Like yeast, this kind of unbelief spreads to all it touches.

Their murmuring differed from David's transparency before God. In his pain, David cried out in distress, and God heard his voice (Psalm 55:16-17). Where else could he go with his aching heart but to the One who had power to heal and save?

David set his eyes on the all-sufficient God, not on the circumstances. His words sprang from a heart of faithfulness, not resistance, to the ways of God. In God, he found cleansing and could conclude his prayer with hope: "Cast your burden upon the Lord, and He will sustain you; He will never allow the righteous to be shaken. . . . I will trust in Thee!" (vv. 22-23)

Single-hearted praise. It is easy to praise God when I see His goodness and feel His presence, but it takes faith to praise Him in times of darkness, loneliness, frustration, and failure. Yet, when I least feel or deserve His loving presence, I most need to praise Him.

The sacrifice of praise flows, not from joyful hearts, but from hearts that know God and long for deeper relationships with their King. These are the "pure in heart," and they shall see beyond all the earthly obstacles to God and His invisible Kingdom (Matthew 5:8). When I choose to love God with all my heart, God's unseen realities become more real than the visible world. When I praise Him for what I neither see nor feel, my King makes those heavenly realities effective in and through my life.

Praise focuses my heart on God. This focus acts like a camera lens set for the horizon—the distant lights of His eternal plan become clearer than the immediate circumstances that crowd me. As I make Him my focal point, the confusions of my life begin to make sense.

My Shepherd promised to complete the work He began in me (Philippians 1:6). Therefore, He trains me to *trust* when I see no results, to *hope* when everything falls apart, to *endure* when the days grow unbearable, and to *praise* when I feel broken and rejected.

All through this process of sanctification, He reminds me that I have died, my self-life was crucified with Jesus. Like David, I am learning to sing, "I have set the Lord continually before me; because He is at my right hand, I will not be shaken" (Psalm 16:8). Hallelujah!

> Let us continually offer up a sacrifice of praise to God, that is, the fruit of lips that give thanks to His name. (Hebrews 13:15)

ᶯ WEARING HIS WARDROBE ᶯ

David's praise sprang from personal experience of the Shepherd's love and power. Read his words of praise. Let them flow through your mind and touch your heart with their truth. Make them your own as you speak them back to God.

Continue to keep a personal journal of God's participation in your life. David "remembered" God's great works and personal love touches. He always had reason to praise because he refused to forget what God had accomplished for him.

Delight in God's names. Each new day brings fresh needs and new ways of discovering God's sufficiency. Do you need direction? He is your Shepherd who shows the way. Do you need peace and purity? He who lives in you is your Peace and Righteousness. Do you need a friend? He is the one Friend who always understands, cares, and acts on your behalf. Praise Him, and you will not only know Him, but also who you are in Him.

Sing praises to Him. Most find it easier to memorize songs than Scriptures. Songs affirm the truths I need to remember. They deepen my awareness of God's unceasing love. During sleepless nights, they soothe me with His presence while they silence Satan's scheme to disturb my thoughts and disrupt my peace in Jesus.

Cultivate the habit of seeing God everywhere. Let His creation remind you of His wonderful attributes. Trees point heavenward in praise of their Maker. Flowers display His love for beauty. Mountains manifest His eternal majesty and crashing waves shout of His power. Ask Him for eyes to see, a heart to enjoy, a mind to expect wondrous revelation, and words to praise God for all that He is to you.

STANDING FIRM TOGETHER

When God calls you to lead a Bible study, be confident that He also will accomplish it (1 Thessalonians 5:23). Trust Him, not yourself! The smaller and weaker you feel, the more you will draw wisdom and strength from Him, and the greater the joy when you experience His sufficiency.

You don't have to be a teacher to start a Bible study. The Holy Spirit will lead and teach through you. When *you* don't have all the answers, others will enjoy bringing valuable insights to the group. *Together* you learn, love, stand, and grow.

Here are some guidelines:

Pray!

Prepare a place—Create a friendly atmosphere. Have coffee or tea ready. Set chairs in a circle. The leader should face the door, ready to welcome latecomers.

Personal Preparation

☐ Know your identity in Christ. Know your resources in Him.

☐ Spend time alone with your Shepherd. His life will flow out of your intimate fellowship with Him to love and nurture others (John 15:4-11).

☐ Before your class meets, let Him search your heart and remove any hindrances to the flow of His Spirit through you. Then trust that He "will be with your mouth and teach you what you should say" (Exodus 4:12; John 14:25-27).

Your First Meeting

☐ Name tags and introductions help break down barriers. Let the group know you. Help them know, love, and trust each other.

☐ Reassure the group that you, their leader, are learning along with them. No one has all the answers.

☐ Share your vision for the group and for its individual members.

☐ Introduce the format for the meetings. You might begin with worship, then discuss the lesson. Personal sharing can be included in lesson applications. Finish with sharing and prayer.

☐ Encourage your group members to complete their lessons at home. Their time alone each day with Jesus, seeking and receiving fresh insights from Him, will make the lessons lively and life-changing.

☐ Encourage each group member to keep a daily journal of prayers, victories, and responses to the suggestions in "Wearing His Wardrobe."

☐ Present guidelines for personal sharing in the group: Be discreet. Never dishonor spouses, parents, children, or friends.

☐ Close with prayer. It is best if only *you* pray the first time, so that no one feels pressured.

Lead through the Lesson

☐ Start promptly; finish on time. The lesson should take no more than an hour. Set aside an additional half hour for sharing, prayer, and fellowship.

☐ Beginning with prayer and a song unites the group in a common focus on God and creates an attitude of worship. You could also pray through a hymn or psalm.

☐ Encourage everyone to participate.

☐ Let group members share their most meaningful answers. Answering around a circle often causes people to be distracted with their individual question rather than listening to one another.

☐ Encourage appropriate sharing on personal questions by setting an example. This helps make the lesson alive, practical, and remembered.

☐ Listen attentively. Receive each answer with appreciation—a smile, thanks, or a sincere compliment; otherwise some will cease to answer. Remember, few questions have a single correct answer.

☐ Close with prayer.

❧ LEADER'S GUIDE 1 ❧

Objective
To help group members begin to envision a way to attain the goal of a life of freedom and victory in Christ.

Personal Preparation
☐ Complete the study, answering all the questions.
☐ Read "Wearing His Wardrobe." Begin your own personal journal with a list of Scriptures to match each area of personal struggle and weakness. Encourage your group members to do the same.
☐ Ask God to make your need and His provision very real to you, so that you can communicate the excitement and privilege of what He offers you. Because most of us tend to seek easy answers and immediate results, it is important to take time to build an awareness of "the joy set before" us. Then we will "press on" toward the lifestyle that produces daily victories (Hebrews 12:2).

Group Participation
☐ Question 2. Point out that whenever we focus on God's exhortations, the Holy Spirit is our Enabler. We follow His guidelines by His strength, not our own. Refer to 2 Corinthians 3:5-6 and 12:9, reminding the group that weakness is an opportunity to receive God's strength. Explain that God's repetitions imply special importance.
☐ Questions 7 and 8. Parts of these questions will be covered in greater depth in later chapters. Let group members know that a complete answer is not expected at this time.
☐ Question 13. Give group members a vision for the type of mutual love, support, and caring you want to see in this group. Without overwhelming them with responsibilities, summarize the messages of the following Scriptures: John 15:12-17; 17:21-23; 1 Corinthians 12:14-27.

❧ *LEADER'S GUIDE 2* ❧

Objective
To help group members know and appropriate truth as the foundation
of a life of freedom and victory in Christ.

Personal Preparation
   ☐ Complete your own study of questions and the narrative.
   ☐ Follow the suggestions in "Wearing His Wardrobe." Ask God to
give you wisdom to discern God's truth from man's information in your
daily activities. Be aware of what kinds of information your mind stores
and your heart absorbs. Your personal example and sharing will help
the others to identify and understand things that influence their
thoughts and attitudes.

Group Participation
   ☐ Question 6. Encourage group members to begin each day by
choosing a similar passage which points to God's greatness and praying
it back to God. The psalms are full of such affirming truths.
   ☐ Question 7. For additional insight, review "Putting on His Word."
   ☐ Question 8. Discuss the two complimentary truths that should be
affirmed before God: God's sufficiency and our need for Him.
   ☐ Remind group members to continue storing up "swords"—Scriptures that affirm and make God's victory effective in every
circumstance.

🎵 *LEADER'S GUIDE 3* 🎵

Objective
To help group members understand, accept, appropriate, and live the righteousness of Jesus.

Personal Preparation
☐ Complete your own study of questions and the narrative.

☐ Spend time in the presence of the King. Let the Holy Spirit bring awareness of any hindrance to the flow of His life into and through you.

☐ Follow the suggestions in "Wearing His Wardrobe." Let the truths of His righteousness be constant reminders of your own identity and worth. Be ready to share how they have made a difference in your own life this week. Discuss what happened when you spoke the truth (your sword) against discouraging thoughts.

☐ Thank God often for giving you His life, purity, and love.

Group Participation
☐ Question 1. Ask each group member to respond to this question. Point out that it is intended to stir a hunger and thirst for all that God wants to share with them. Note that when we are aware of our need, God's sufficiency becomes all the more precious.

☐ Questions 4 and 5. Have your group compare this righteousness to that of the Pharisees in Matthew 5:20 and Mark 7:1-8.

🍂 *LEADER'S GUIDE 4* 🍂

Objective
To help group members understand and experience God's peace.

Personal Preparation
☐ Complete your own study of the questions and the narrative.
☐ Practice the meditation in "Wearing His Wardrobe." Be ready to share your times of seeking and finding God's peace in unpeaceful circumstances.

Group Participation
☐ Question 1. Encourage group members to take time to look at the Shepherd. Pray through the Psalm 23. Then share insights from the meditation in "Wearing His Wardrobe."
☐ Question 2. Help your group gain a deeper understanding by comparing these points with James 1:6-7.
☐ Question 12. Have group members discuss *how* they can help each other affirm their identities, and *why* it is important to do so.
☐ Continue to encourage the group to collect "swords."

❧ *LEADER'S GUIDE 5* ❧

Objective
To help group members know the basis of their faith and live in that
faith continually.

Personal Preparation
☐ Complete your own study of the questions. Pay special attention
to the personal questions. Make the suggested observations yourself,
and be ready to share with the class what God has shown you.
☐ Write your observations as suggested in "Wearing His
Wardrobe."

Group Participation
☐ Question 1. In your review of the armor, have the group discuss
the significance of the armor as a whole, of the sequence of the pieces,
and of each individual part. Encourage group members to exercise
their faith by "putting on the whole armor" every day.
☐ Question 12. Have the group look at the way Jesus responded to
the challenges in His earthly life. Ask: **How did His attitudes and
actions demonstrate faith?**

❧ LEADER'S GUIDE 6 ❧

Objective
To help group members understand and live their salvation in a daily, practical way.

Personal Preparation
☐ Follow the practical suggestions in "Putting on His Word." Then you will be ready to illustrate answers to questions with fresh examples from your own life.

☐ Follow the suggestions in "Wearing His Wardrobe." Notice how your written communion with God deepens your relationship with Him. Be ready to share your growth with the group.

Group Participation
☐ Question 2. Your group will have a variety of answers to this question. Share the following possible answer with your group: **Because He has called us into His Kingdom and purpose, we have confident, expectant hope for this and every day. Because we share His inheritance, we have abundant resources to meet every challenge. Because we share His infinite power, we need never fear.**

☐ Remind the group to prepare their "swords"—the Scriptures that will affirm God's power and victory in every personal area of temptation and struggle.

❧ LEADER'S GUIDE 7 ❧

Objective

To help group members see the sword of God's Word as essential to victory.

Personal Preparation

☐ Complete your own study of questions and the narrative.

☐ Practice the suggestions in "Wearing His Wardrobe."

☐ Be ready to share your own collection of Scripture swords. Be prepared to motivate each participant to seek and discover Scriptures appropriate to personal needs and weaknesses.

Group Participation

☐ Review each piece of armor, its sequence, significance, and application. Invite personal sharing. Affirm the various ways group members have put on the armor.

☐ Ask group members to share their swords and their effectiveness in battle. Learn from each other. One person's sword may be God's exhortation to another.

☐ Question 3. Spend some time looking together at the King in Revelation 19:11-16. Discuss and delight in His majesty, power, and names. Emphasize that He is the mighty Word of God! He is the King of Kings, and Lord of Lords! This mighty sovereign God is the One who loves and covers us! Encourage the group to see the wealth and wonder of what they have in Christ.

Faithful + true
Word of God
King of Kings
Lord of lords

🍂 *LEADER'S GUIDE 8* 🍂

Objective
To help group members understand and practice the power of praise.

Personal Preparation
☐ Complete your own study of questions and the narrative.
☐ Follow the suggestions in "Wearing His Wardrobe."
☐ Ask God to make you alert to the effectiveness of praise in your own life. Be ready to share your struggles and victories with the group.

Group Participation
☐ Question 1. Encourage your group to discover God's armor not only in Psalm 18, but throughout the Bible by memorizing their favorite sections. It will bring protection and victory, for it secures the whole armor.
☐ Question 4. Discuss both verses. Encourage group members to add these wonderful prayers to their collection of swords.
☐ Question 5. Encourage each group member to share the *one* truth about God that means the most to her today.
☐ Question 6. Give group members opportunity to share *one* things about themselves that points to their need for God. Remind them that their weakness and need opens the door to God's sufficiency and triumph (2 Cor. 12:9-10).